THE MEASURE OF MY STRENGTH

UZINGA LEMANDLA AMI

THE MEASURE OF MY STRENGTH

LIZINGA LEMANDLA AMI

SUNNI MERCER

BRIDGET & ERIC PIPKIN

KIRKPATRICK FOUNDATION, INC.

Tate Publishing & *Enterprises*

Published by Tate Publishing & Enterprises, LLC
127 E. Trade Center Terrace | Mustang, Oklahoma 73064 USA
1.888.361.9473 | www.tatepublishing.com

Tate Publishing is committed to excellence in the publishing industry. The company reflects the philosophy established by the founders, based on Psalm 68:11,
"The Lord gave the word and great was the company of those who published it."

Sculpture, Stories and Narratives by Sunni Mercer
Photography by Bridget and Eric Pipkin
Sculpture Photography by Ann Sherman
Editing by Michelle Meisner
Cover & interior design by Leah LeFlore

Published in the United States of America

ISBN: 978-1-61739-633-5
1. Art, Collections, Catalogs, Exhibitions
10.08.31

DEDICATION

This book is dedicated to our families—your unwavering support and love is a blessing beyond measure.

And to all the precious women and children in Swaziland—you graciously let us enter into your world; your lives. We may never see you again, but your image; your story will burn in our hearts forever.

Sunni Mercer
Bridget and Eric Pipkin

TABLE OF CONTENTS

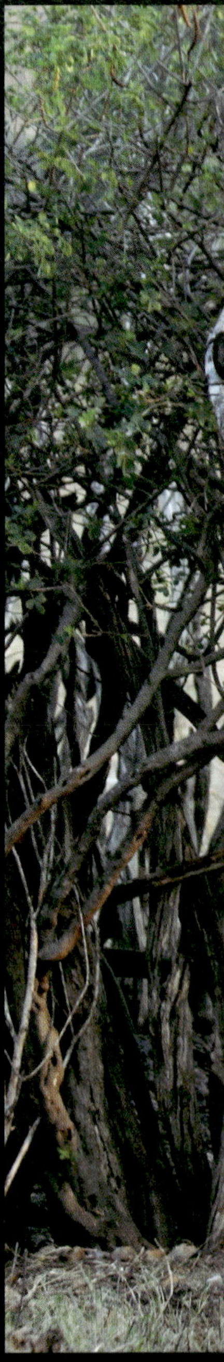

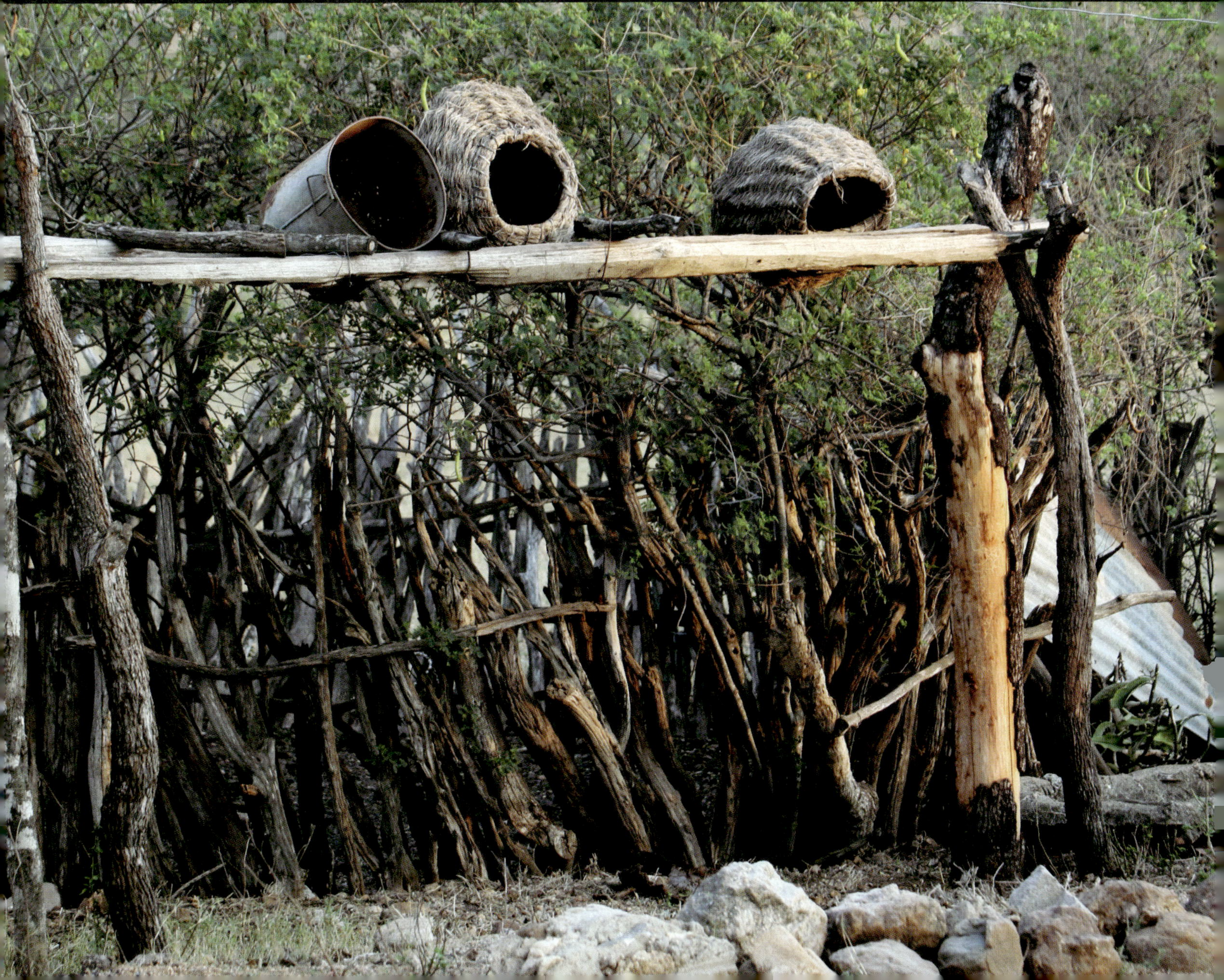

FOREWORD

Loren P. Gresham, President, Southern Nazarene University
David Busic, Senior Pastor, Bethany First Church of the Nazarene

This book tells compelling individual stories about the power of hope and the strength of endurance in the face of profound and devastating hardship.

The women of Swaziland have much to teach us. They face challenges and difficulties daily as they care for the children left abandoned by victims of the AIDS epidemic, yet their words and images testify to perseverance, hope, and joy. By stepping across the generations that have been broken by disease and death, they forge a tangible link to the future of their families and their country. Their strength has become a conduit of grace for the brokenness surrounding them.

Through the Church of the Nazarene, Oklahomans have been part of the corporate story in Swaziland for more than a century. Today's Swaziland Partnership is a cooperative effort between the Swaziland Church of the Nazarene, Bethany First Church of the Nazarene, and Southern Nazarene University, focused on reducing the incidence of HIV/AIDS in Swaziland by developing key spiritual, compassionate, and educational resources.

Art, and love, have the power to evoke our compassion and connect us to others across time and place. We invite you to encounter and reflect on the moving and inspiring words and images in this book. You will find your own spirit inspired by the faith and courage of the women you will meet.

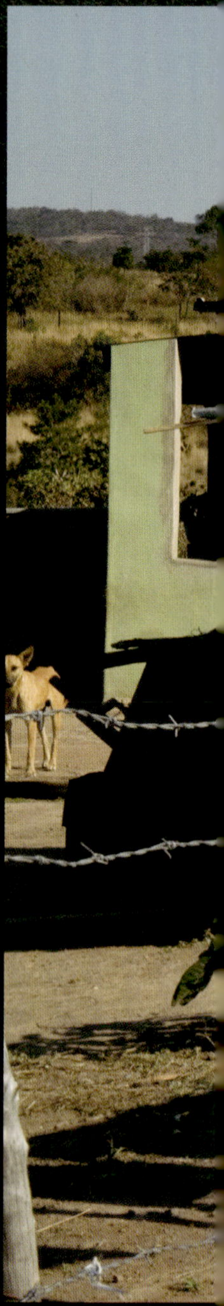

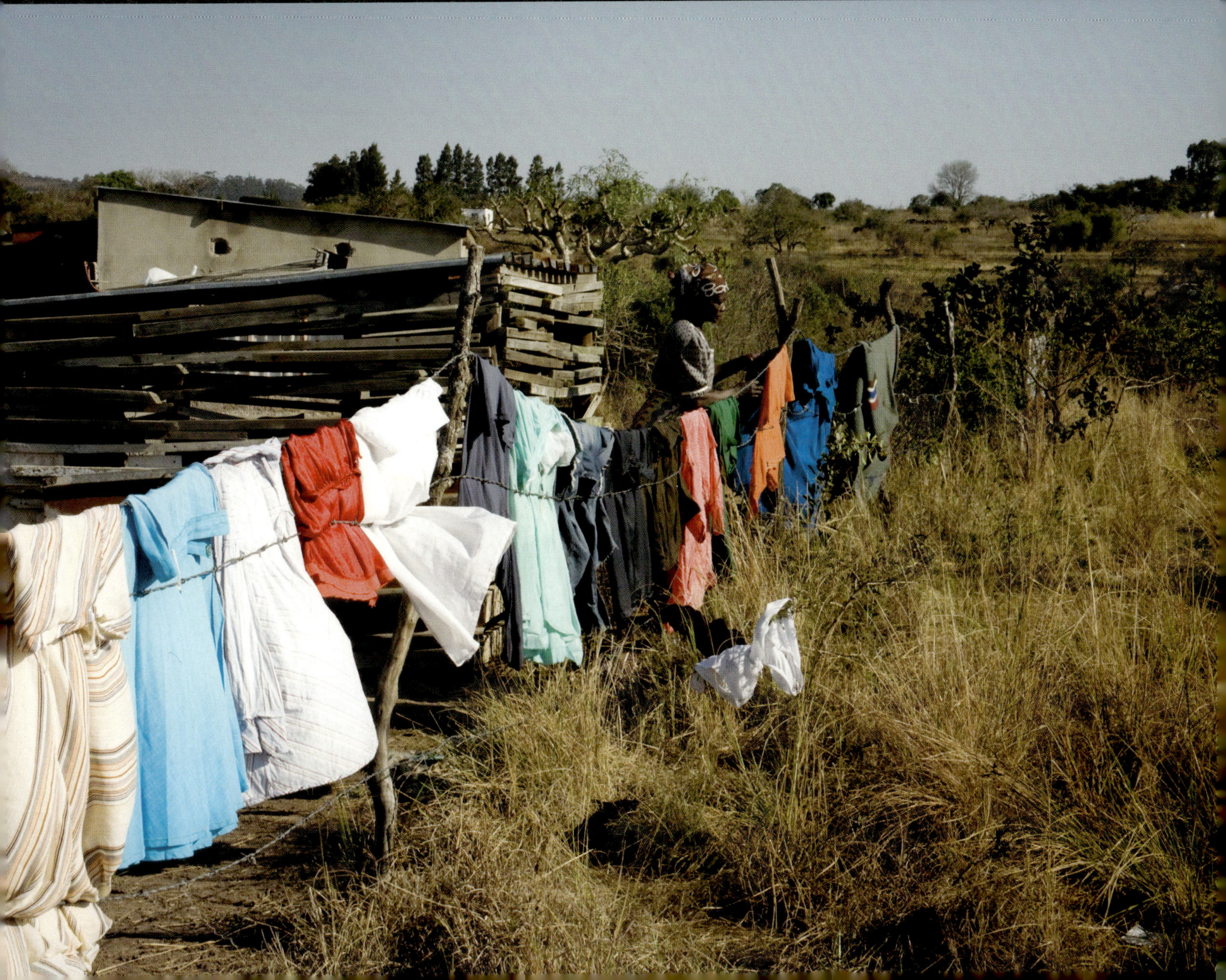

INFORMATION ON SWAZILAND

Swaziland is not as big as you might imagine, and comparatively speaking, is slightly smaller than New Jersey. Swaziland is only about 10,500 square miles, making it the smallest country in the southern hemisphere. It is a landlocked nation surrounded primarily by South Africa and neighbored on the east by Mozambique. Its temperate and subtropical climate brings very hot summer temperatures well above 75 degrees Fahrenheit and winter temperatures of 59 degrees and higher. Swaziland's terrain is comprised mostly of mountains and hills with many sloping plains and a variety of flora and fauna. It is a country with a limited food supply, including a depleted supply of animals due to hunting, and a shortage of portable water. Much of Swaziland's soil is eroded due to overgrazing, degradation, flooding, and drought, which also contribute to the food problems. It is a total monarchy and is ruled by King Mswati III, who took power in 1986. Swaziland ranks as a lower middle-income country, and more than half of its population—nearly one million people—live in poverty.

Medical practices are also a big concern in Swaziland. Although herbal medical practices are common, these herbal remedies, which come from various types of plants, are not diagnosed through scientific research and, therefore, offer no documentation of medical practice success. Because of this, practitioners have no proof of the effectiveness of herbal medicine, which has been used for generations to treat illnesses as simple as headaches to complicated diseases such as AIDS. These traditional practices are the main source and delivery of primary healthcare in Swaziland. Approximately 85% of the population relies on these practices exclusively, and the acceptance of these practices is mainly due to cultheir beliefs about traditional medicine. Herbal medicine is also popular because it is much more affordable by the general population than conventional drugs, which are too expensive for most people.

Swaziland also has a strong traditional religious heritage. Their Supreme Being, who they believe ultimately formed the Earth, requires no worship or sacrifices and is known to them as Mkhulumnqande. However, ancestral spirits are a big part of Swazi culture. Both men and women take great responsibility in keeping these spirits, who they believe influence them, content. It is believed by the people that these ancestral spirits take on many forms, sometimes possessing people, and sometimes influencing their health or welfare. The people want to keep these ancestors, whom they believe to be among them, happy at all costs. The ancestral spirits are considered responsible for rain and many common diseases. The spirits of the deceased are also believed to be able to present themselves as snakes, inflicting suffering on their descendants as rightful punishment to correct wrong behavior, but the spirits never inflict suffering out of anger. Because of these beliefs, Swazi women are given the role of communicating with these spirits. The head of the household in each Swazi home is expected to sacrifice offerings to ancestors at important events such as deaths, births, and new marriages, to keep the peace and alleviate any bad omens that may exist between the people and their ancestors. In this small nation, traditional Swazi medicine works so perfectly with accepted religious beliefs that new methods, including western medical practices, become suspect.[1,2,3]

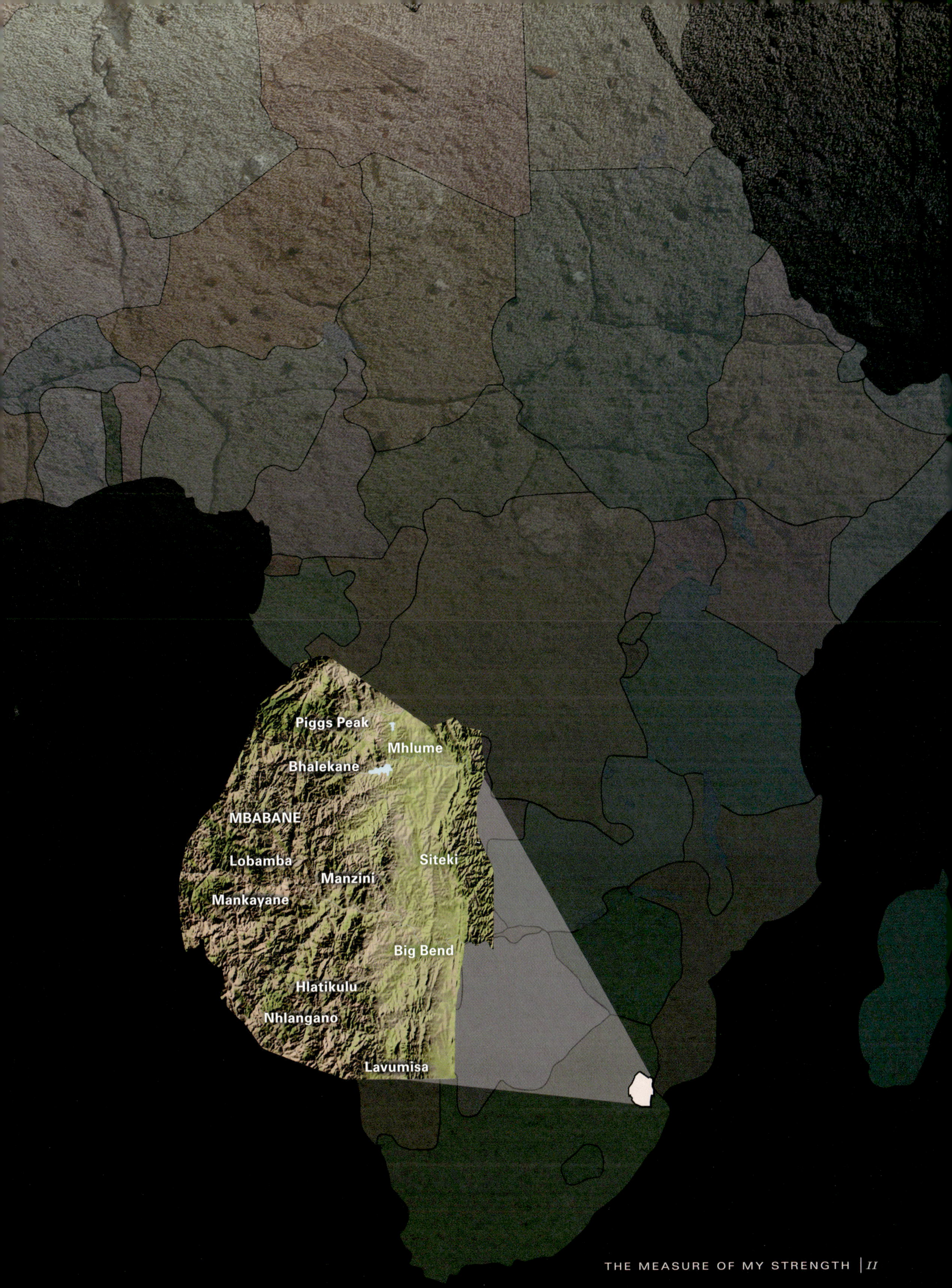
Piggs Peak
Mhlume
Bhalekane
MBABANE
Lobamba
Siteki
Manzini
Mankayane
Big Bend
Hlatikulu
Nhlangano
Lavumisa

RECIPIENTS

The Swaziland HIV/AIDS Task Force

The HIV/AIDS Task Force offers home-based care for people who suffer from HIV/AIDS, disabilities, or other terminal illnesses. The Task Force provides support groups for those who are HIV positive. Some groups have developed their own co-operative vegetable gardens to provide food and financial support. Currently, there are 112 caregivers who visit clients at least once a week. Through these caregivers, more than 400 clients from all over the country are provided for on a monthly basis. To date, more than 200 orphans (with numbers growing daily) and vulnerable children are helped through the Task Force. The care provided for all HIV/AIDS Task Force clients range from: provision of food, personal goods, home health care, emotional and spiritual support, counseling, and encouragement to obtain and maintain ARV treatment, and some educational sponsorship for orphans..

Gigi's Place

Gigi's Place operates a free preschool and a feeding program for preschool street children. Five days a week, approximately 320 vulnerable children and Task Force clients are served a meal, usually consisting of rice and mealie meal with gravy. Currently, there is very little meat or vegetables available—something the Task Force would like to change. When the children are ready for further education, the staff helps them attend primary school. Gigi's Place is located in the Ka-Khoza area of Manzini, Swaziland. It was started by the HIV/AIDS Task Force and a local businesswoman. Currently there are approximately 10 or fewer volunteers who staff the daily operations. The Children's Cup, a local charity, also helped to provide initial funding and basic food in connection with NERCHA.

The Morningstar Institute

The Morningstar Institute, founded by Southern Nazarene University and housed in the SNU School of Business, educates students about international development and poverty alleviation, including practical training through international internships. Morningstar Institute interns began working in Swaziland in the summer of 2010 with the HIV/AIDS Task Force community gardens project. This project grew out of the Swazi ministry called the HIV/AIDS Task Force, a vital component of the community-centric response to AIDS. Community gardens have been started in various rural areas of Swaziland and have been tended by support groups of Task Force patients who have become well enough to undertake gardening to support their families and community. Morningstar Institute student interns will work with the Task Force to review preparations for the gardens to become self-sustaining and to evaluate their impact, especially how these gardens can generate extra produce to finance needs such as school fees. The interns will measure the gardens' progress and success at various stages of their development. One of the garden sites that Morningstar interns will assess is in the community of Luve. This is one of the first garden sites with the Task Force and is the size of a large farm. In an academic partnership between SNU and the University of Swaziland, these interns will select two or three of these community gardens to evaluate their impact on the community and to provide essential feedback to the HIV/AIDS Task Force and the donors that help sponsor these gardens.

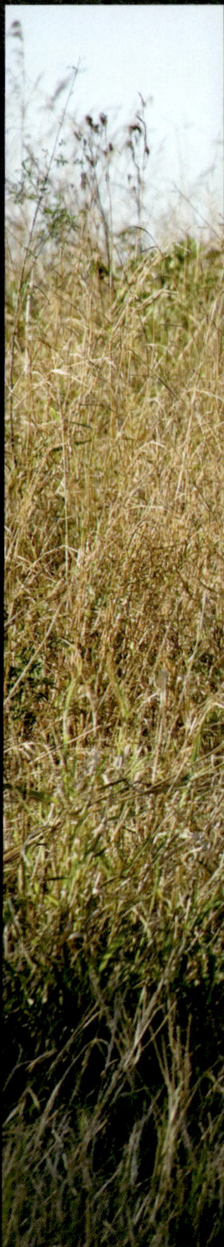

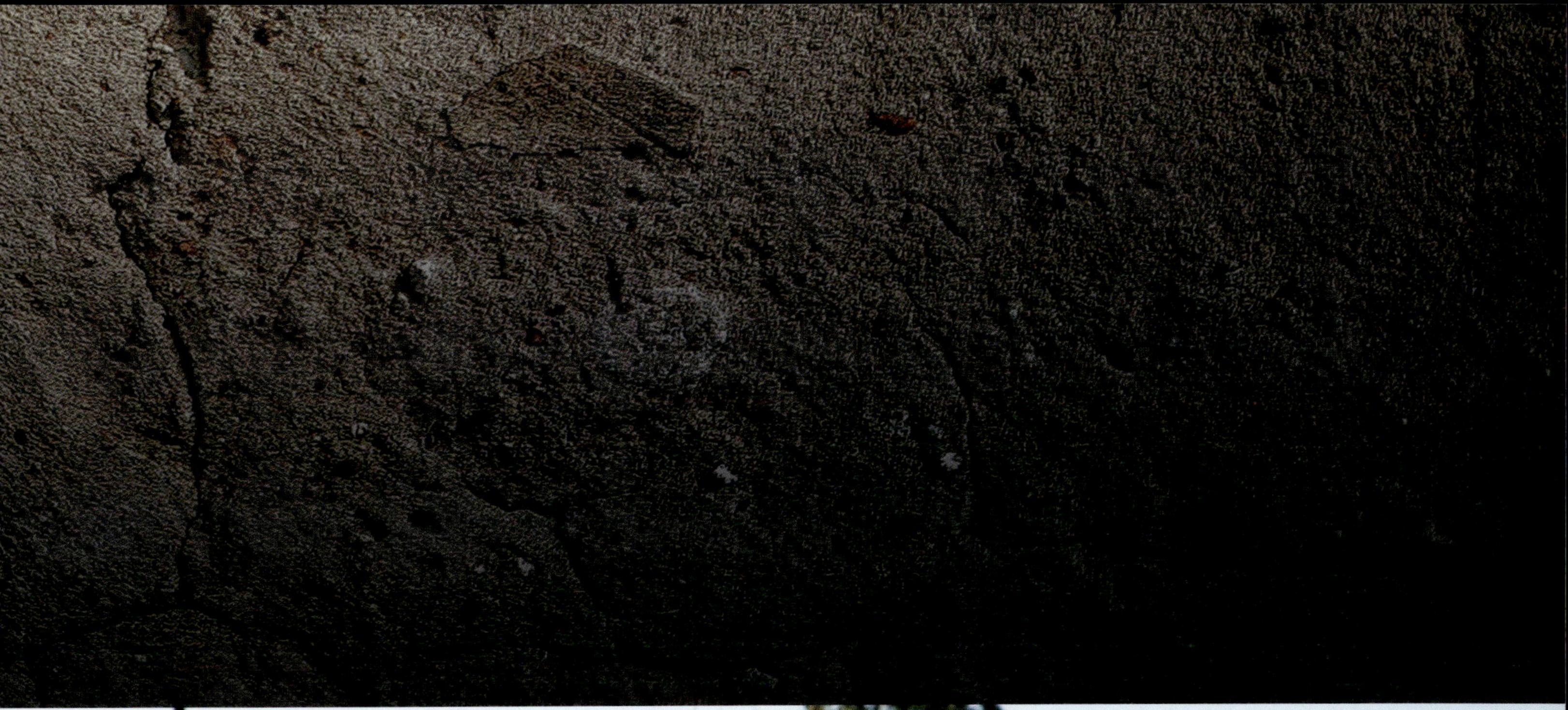

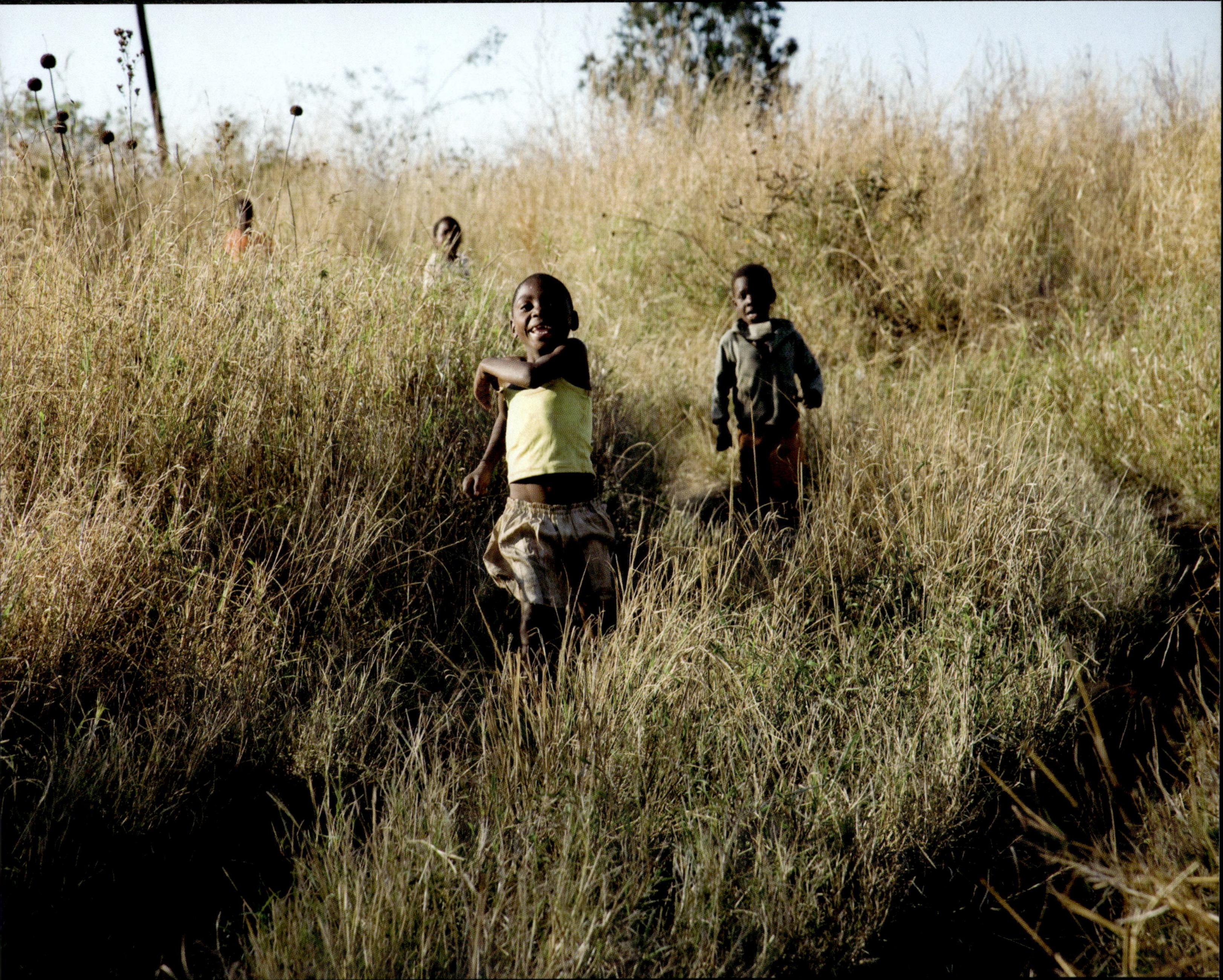

ARTIST STATEMENT

Sunni Mercer

I went to Swaziland to gather research for this exhibit.

What I came back with were lessons in dignity, images of grace.

Swazi women are strong.

Their resilience in the face of seemingly insurmountable odds is astounding.

In a country where disease has penetrated the adult population killing entire generations and leaving thousands of orphaned children behind, the task of survival rests mostly on the shoulders of the women. The daily burden of providing food and caring for their young while nursing the sick and dying is daunting. When the caretaker herself is alone, malnourished, and indigent, the difficulties multiply. Regardless, these indomitable women do not allow their circumstances to seize their love for community nor their capacity for joy.

Swazi women understand the seamlessness of time and the eternity that exists in relationships. They do not fear the loss of things. They fear leaving the ones they love behind. For the women of Swaziland, incredible pain and indelible joy go hand in hand. At the end of the day, around the fire, Swazi "sisters" laugh hard and long. Without the trappings of stuff, they find joy in communion with each other.

They desperately need our assistance—our support—in the areas of healthcare, medicine, water, and nutrition. But the women of Swaziland, these towers of strength, will also give to us; they will teach us all something about the power of community and the freedom found in simplicity. Their stories reflect the resilience of their spirit, their hope for eternity ... the measure of their strength.

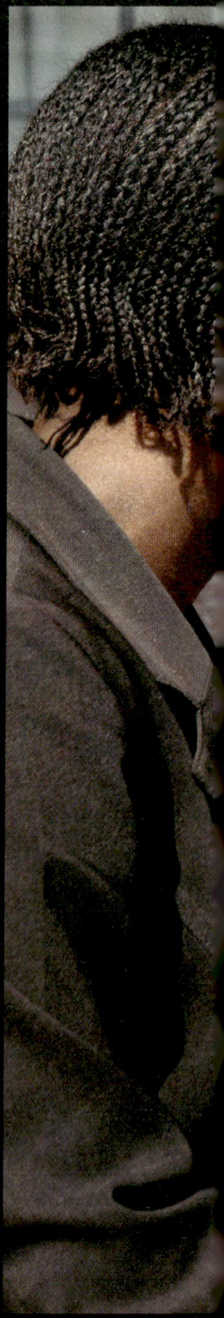

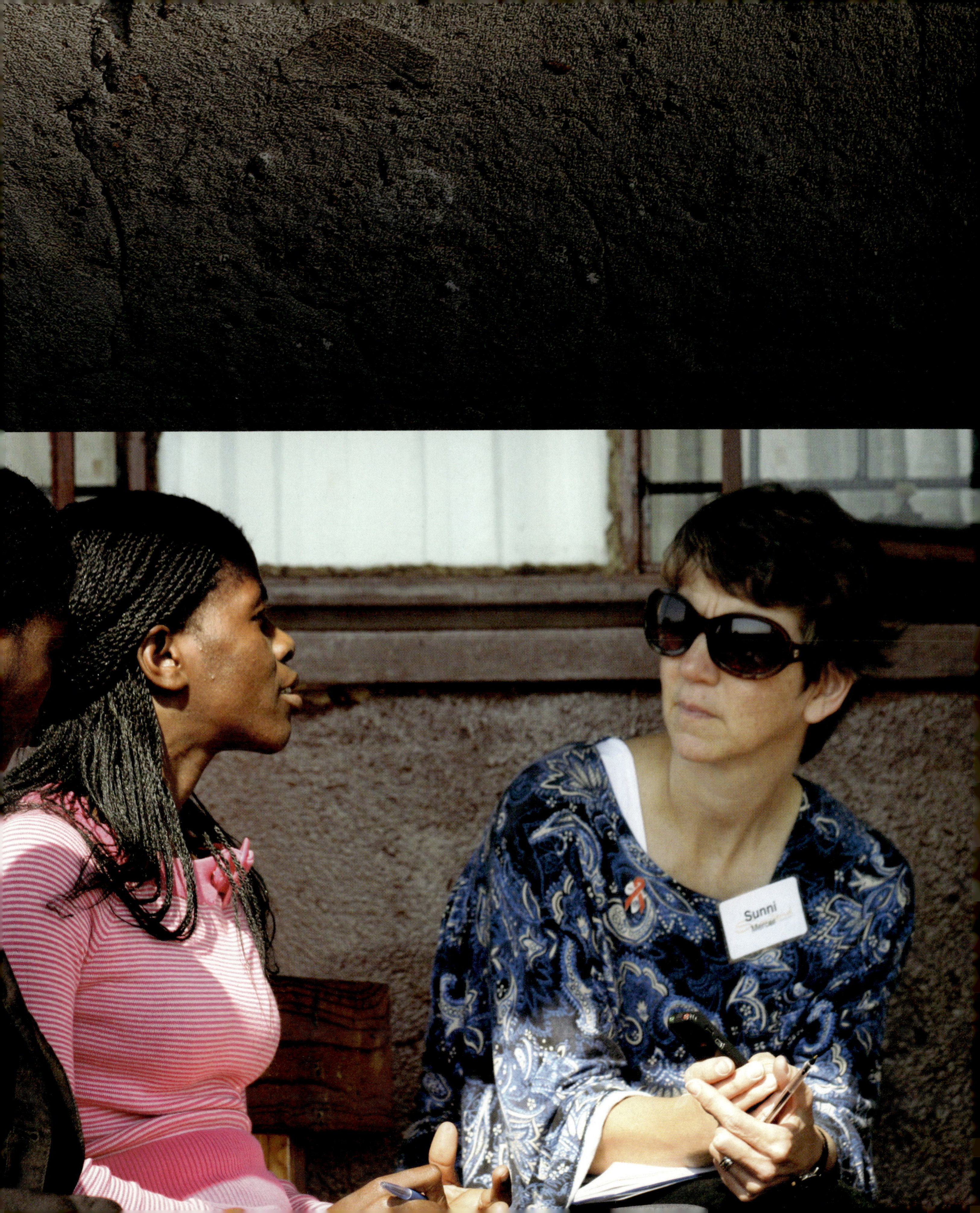
Sunni

LIZINGA LEMANDLA AMI

The Measure of My Strength

The vision to create an exhibit on such a highly charged subject as HIV/AIDS in a "far away" country could not be fully realized from the studio. The goal was to better understand the impact of HIV/AIDS on the women and children of Swaziland, Africa. To this end, we traveled to Swaziland. There, Bridget, Eric, and I witnessed the ravages of the HIV/AIDS pandemic first hand. This horrible virus and all the secondary diseases that prey upon weakened immune systems are killing entire generations of Swazi people.

While in Swaziland, we visited the Raleigh Fitkin Memorial Hospital in Manzini, we traveled with the HIV/AIDS Task Force to visit dying patients living in huts throughout the bush; we visited clinics, markets, and places where children gather for food. We gathered stories and conducted interviews with over 65 women, and captured hundreds of images of women and children as well as the environments in which they live.

Prior to our trip, and long after, I gathered materials for my studio, found objects of all kinds and a vast accumulation of supplies for creating unique assemblages. I researched new techniques for a variety of casting and molding applications while Bridget and Eric reviewed and edited hundreds of images to find the most appropriate storytellers.

After years of development, *Lizinga Lemandla Ami: The Measure of My Strength*, was realized. The resulting interpretive exhibition includes mixed media sculpture, photography, and narrative text panels.

These twelve art objects juxtaposed to the narrative panels and images serve to initiate a dialogue within the viewer. They become *Stations* designed to encourage contemplation, personal reflection, and hopefully motivate a compassionate response within the viewer.

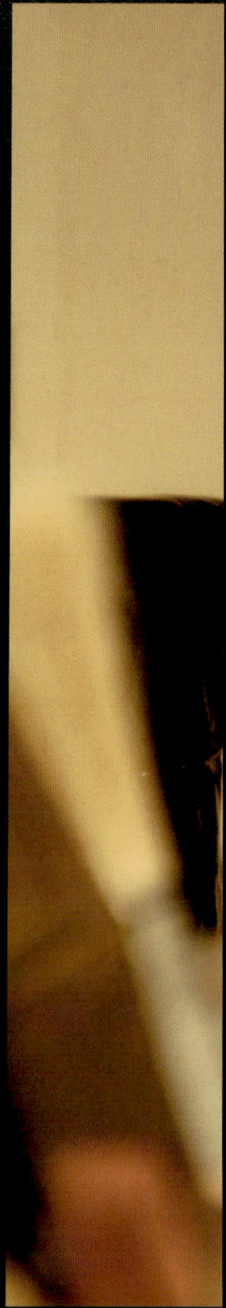

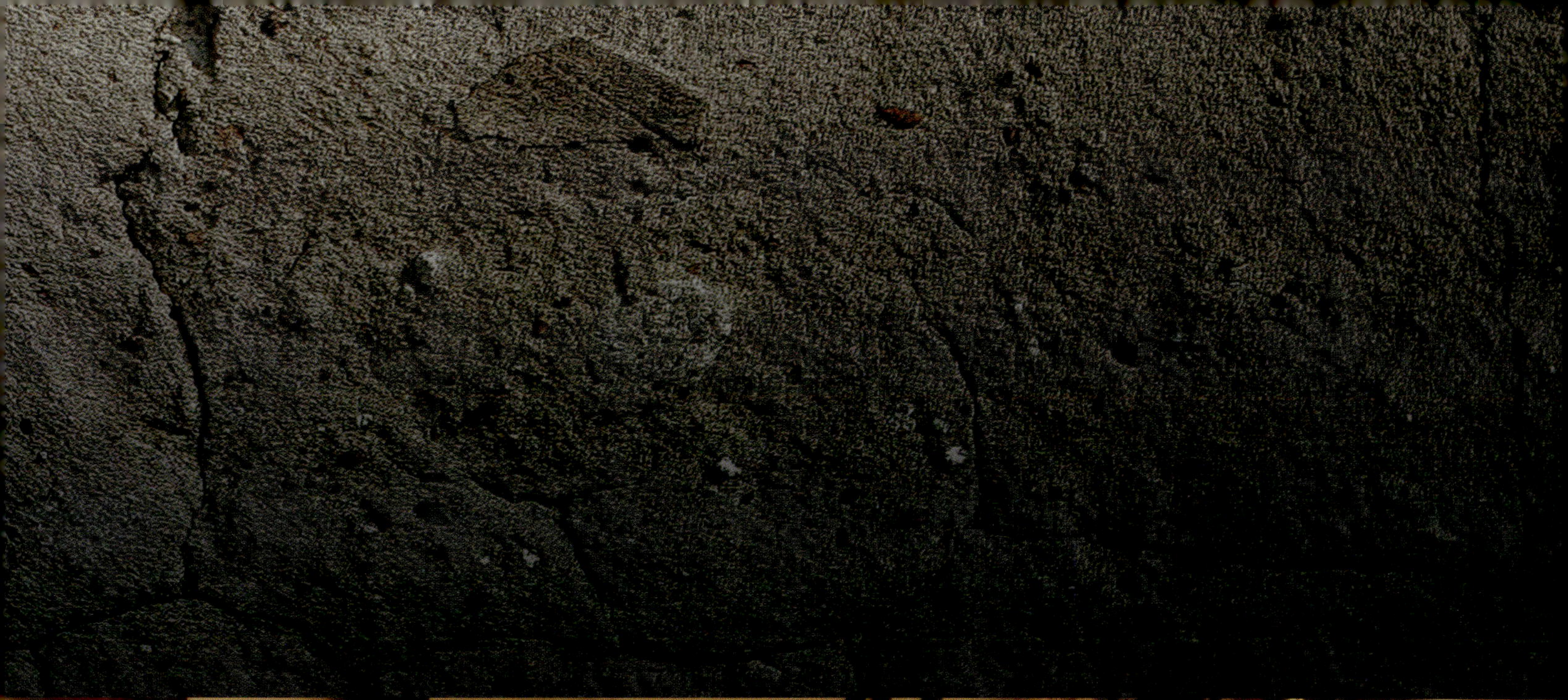

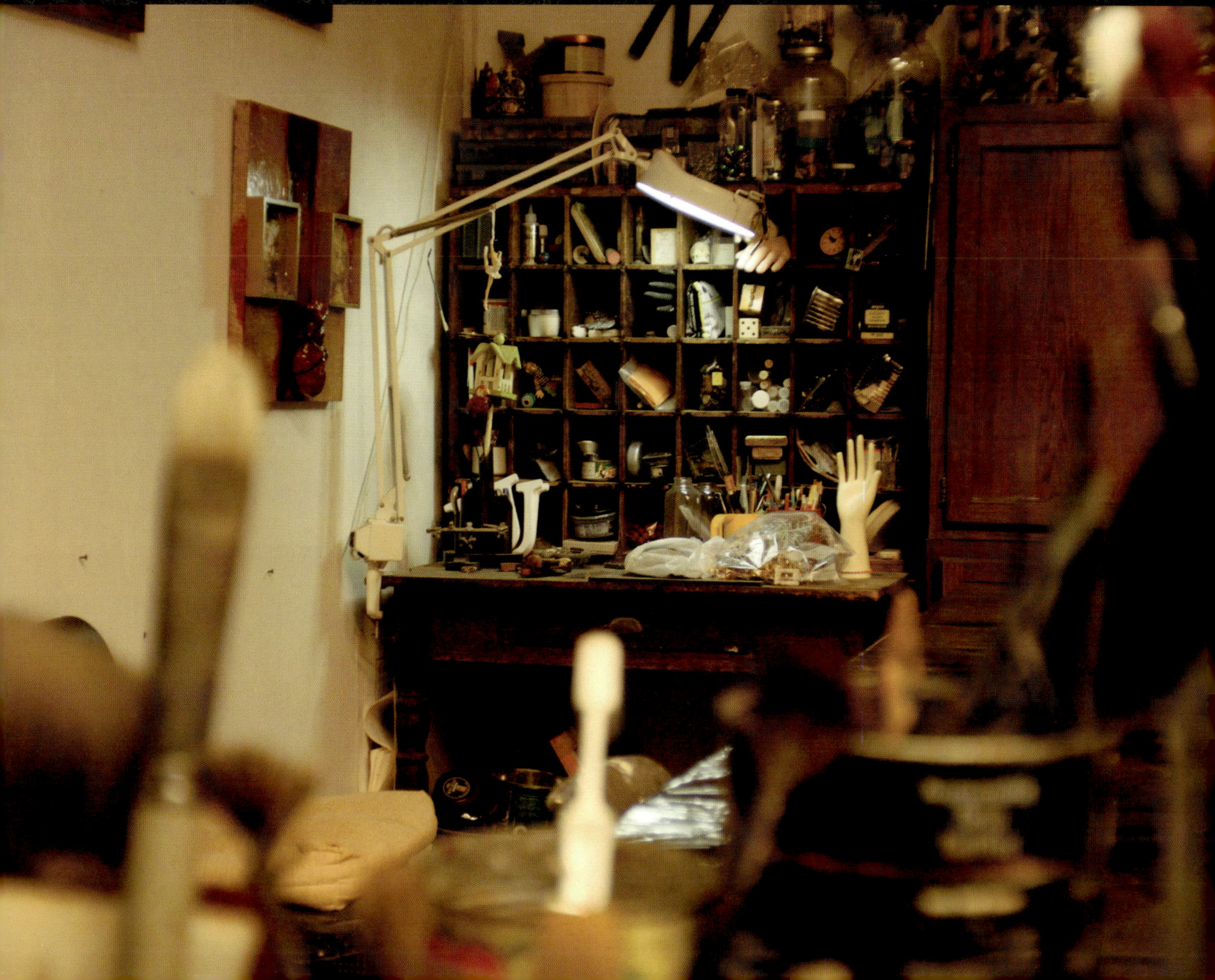

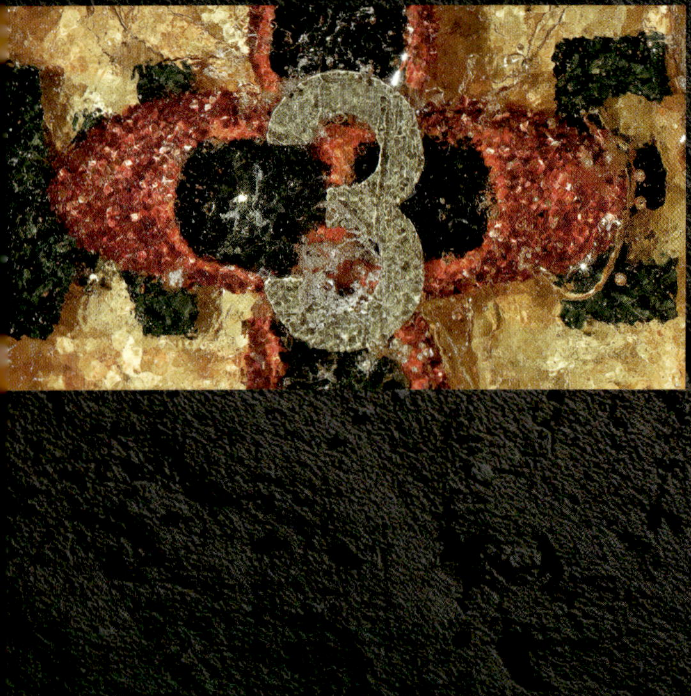
3

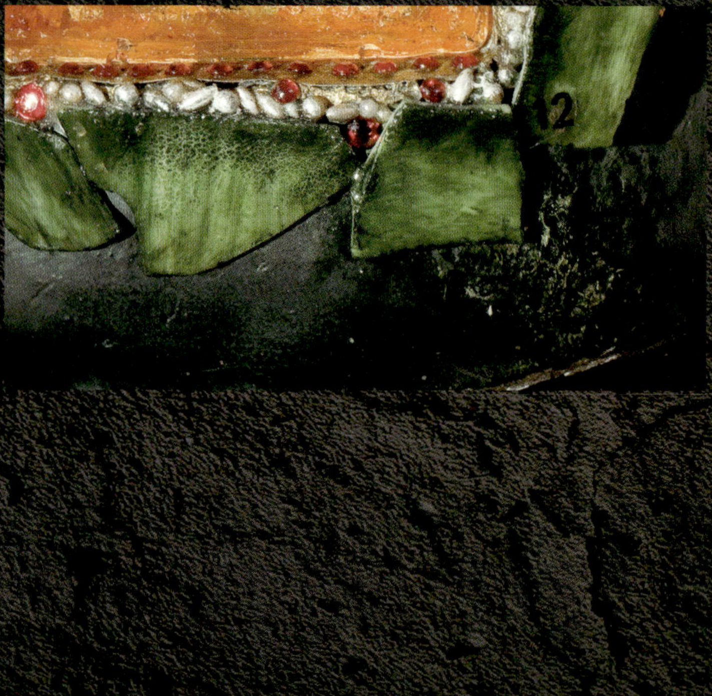
12

"Understanding and tenderness would arise among us no matter how bad things got, and we found redemption in the very places we hurt most."

—LIN JENSEN

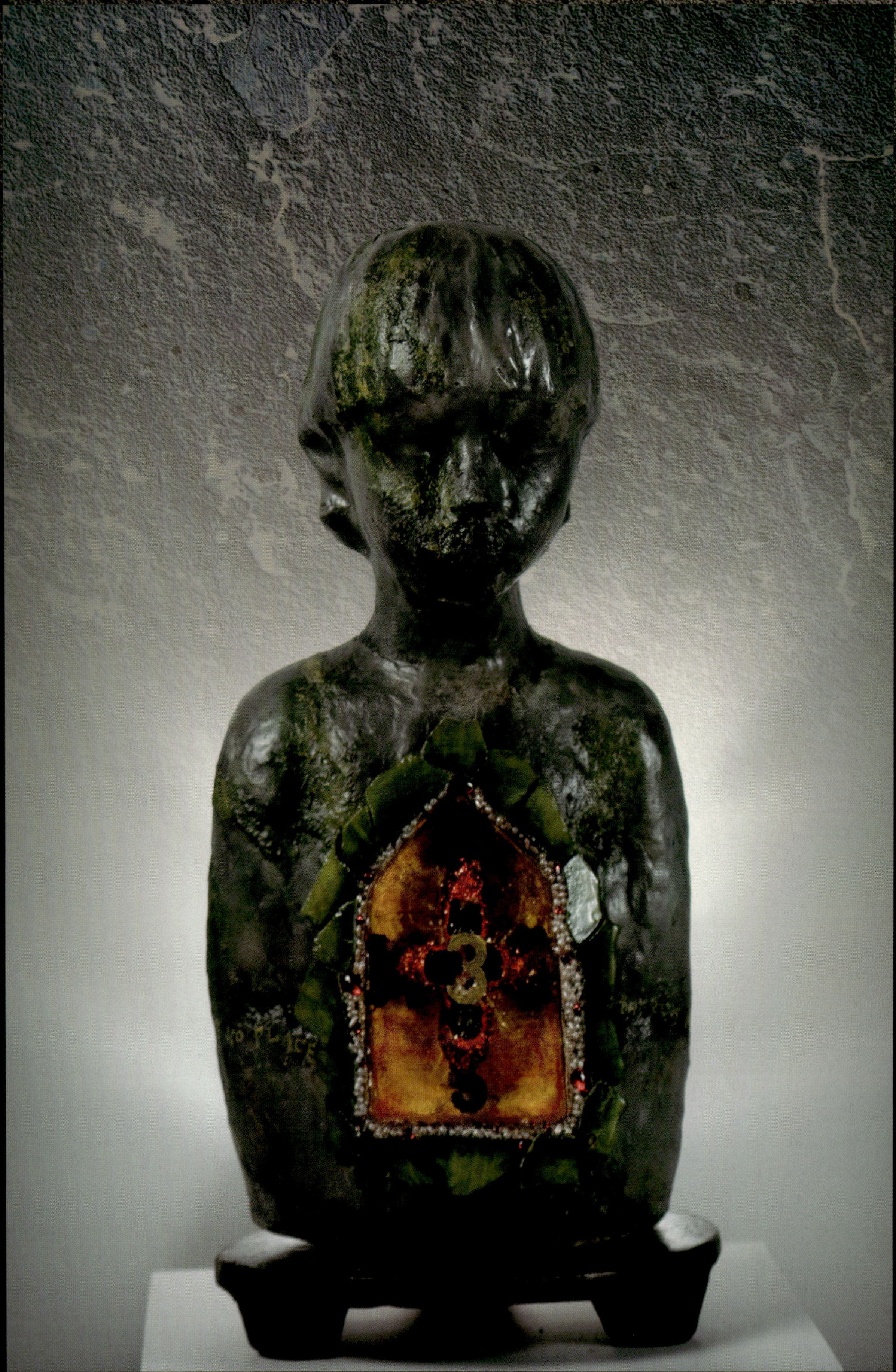

I AM A BOULDER, ALWAYS TUMBLING AND TURNING, LEAVING TRAILS OF SAND AND GRIT ON PATHS OF ERODED RELATIONSHIPS. THE MOSS OF NEED STICKS.

IN A QUEST FOR BELONGING, I DON IMPOTENT RUBY SLIPPERS. HEELLESS THEY ARE POWERLESS. IN THIS PLACE MEASURED BY MY STEPS, "THERE IS NO PLACE LIKE HOME."

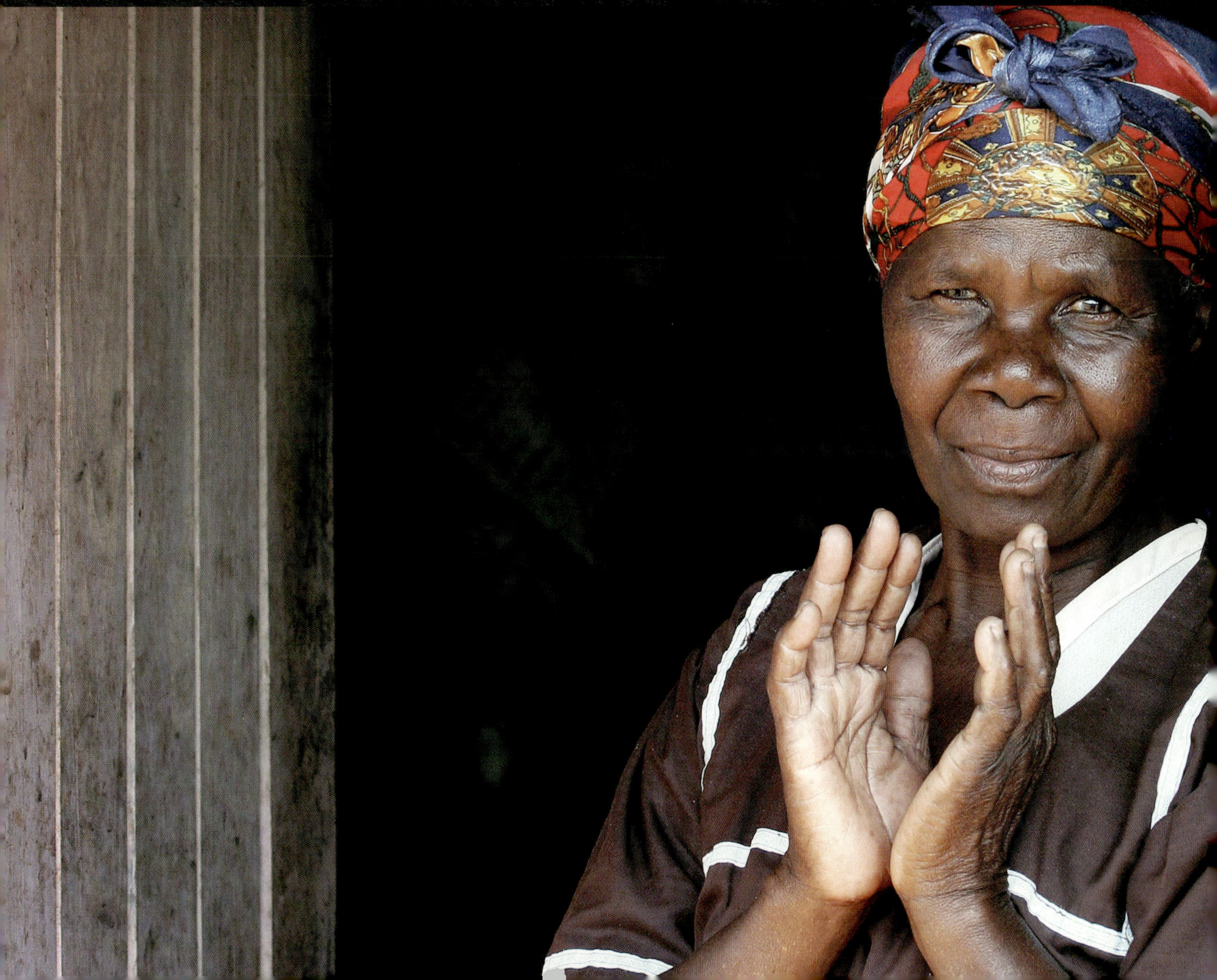

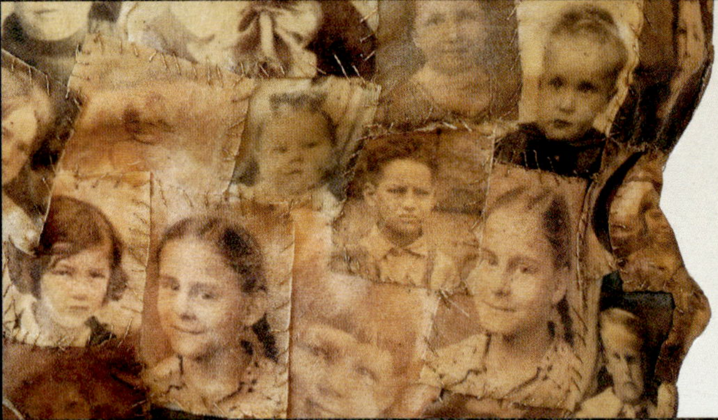

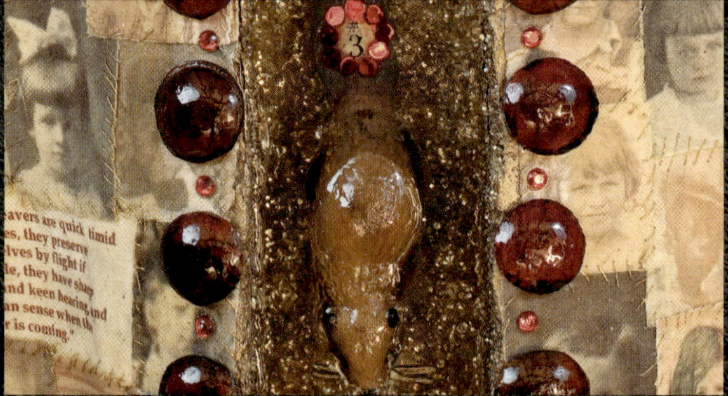
avers are quick timid
es, they preserve
lves by flight if
le, they have sharp
nd keen hearing and
an sense when the
r is coming."
3

"We must stitch up what has been torn apart, render justice imaginable in a world which is so obviously unjust, make happiness meaningful for nations poisoned by the misery of this century. Naturally, it is a superhuman task. But tasks are called superhuman when men take a long time to complete them that is all."

—ALBERT CAMUS

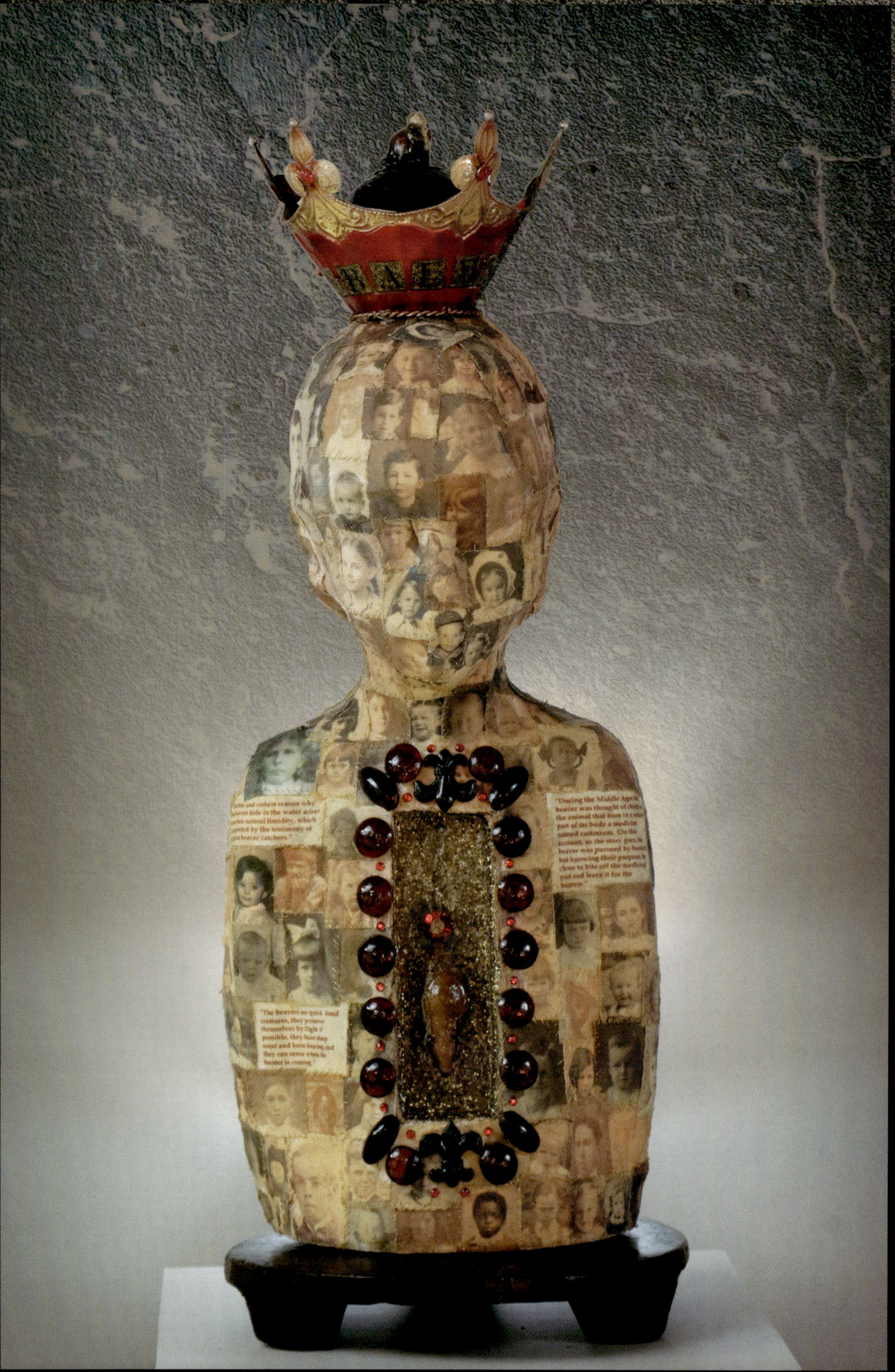

I AM SEWN TO THE PAST; STRANDS OF GOLD HOLD ME TAUT. STORY TO STORY, HEART TO HEART, WE SING A SONG OF KNOWING. WE CHOOSE OUR HIDING PLACES—STRONGHOLDS FROM OUR EARTHLY SEEKERS. REFUGE IN THE COOL OF A DARK CLOSET SHELTER, WE WAIT. STRENGTH OF THE CHILDREN—STRONG RESOLVE— WE TEACH OURSELVES TO SURVIVE. TOGETHER ALONE WE WILL REMAIN UNTIL THE CHAINS THAT SCAR ARE BROKEN.

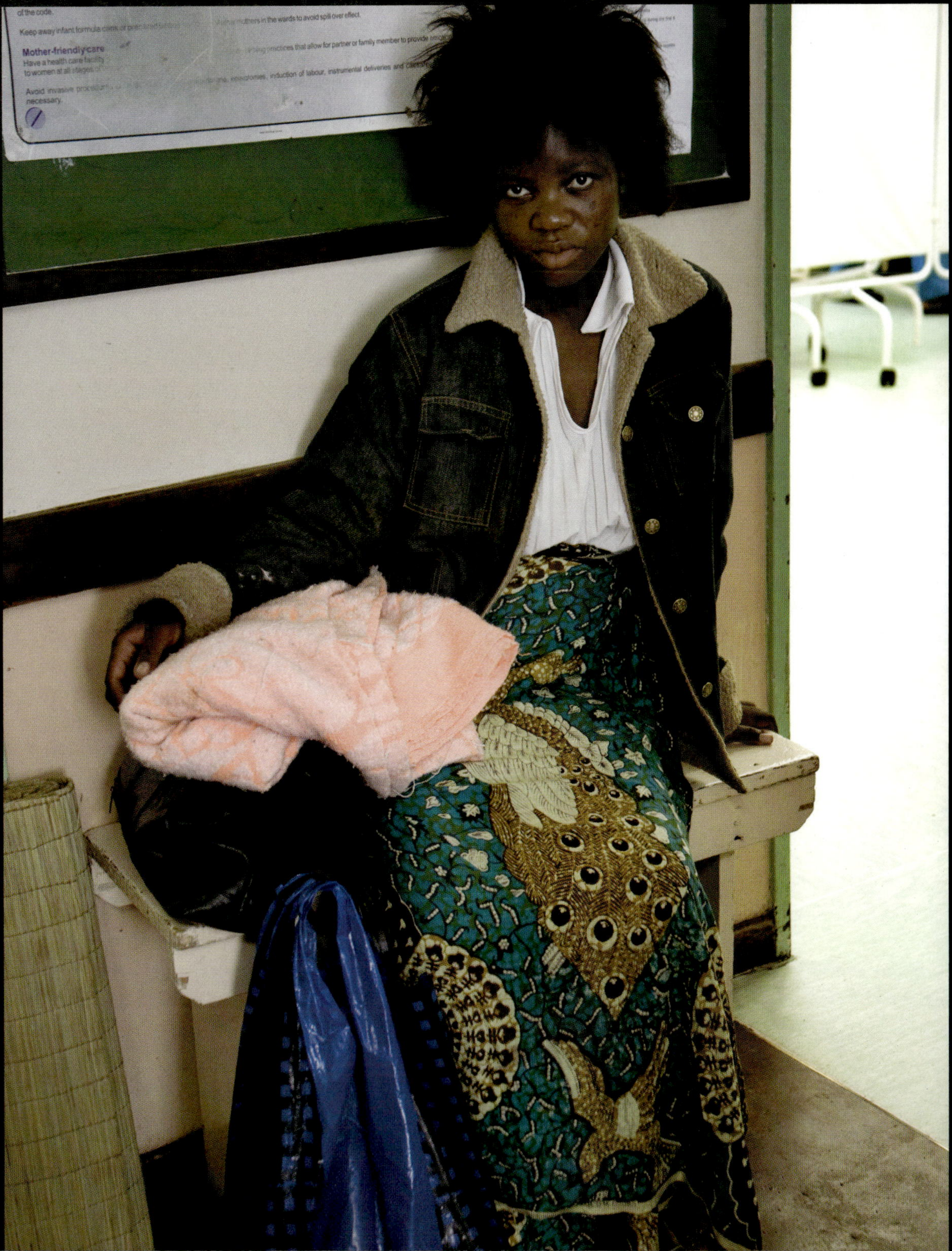

THE ADVOCATES

There are men and women in Swaziland who decide to openly share stories of their struggles with HIV/AIDS. They are referred to as "Expert Clients." They willingly divulge their condition and how they contracted the disease so that others will find the courage to be tested. In a country devastated by the plague of AIDS, Expert Clients are saving lives, one story and one person at a time.

Meet the Twins.

They arrive on the porch for the interview arm in arm. Sitting down next to each other on the bench in the morning sun, they share an energy between them. There is a familial mystery here. They are twins, and this offers an understanding of their bond. Nonni and GuGu are in their mid to late twenties, both beautiful and full of energy. Nonni shares with us.

"I tested when I was pregnant. Here in Swaziland you have to be tested when you get pregnant. My results were positive. It wasn't as hard for me because my sister had gone through this; she had tested before. We thought she would die when they told us but she said, 'No, I will not die.' She helped us understand that 'positive' doesn't mean you will die."

GuGu nods in agreement, stating that when she tested positive she was encouraged to share with others. "I said OK, I can go to the public. I am not afraid." So I went to my family and when they saw me they knew I was not dying. 'You are still GuGu, the one we know,' they said to me. I told them, "Yes, I am not sick, I am just HIV positive."

Now the twins spend their lives sharing with others who are afraid to be tested. Both Nonni and GuGu find hope in helping others. "We tell them, 'You are not going to die. Please go for the test and you will know your status.'" Because Nonni and GuGu come from a wealthy family, their condition helps dispel the myth that only the

"We just want to help our people."

Meet Pumy.

The Luke Commission, a medical mission providing mobile clinics to rural Swaziland, had come to Manzini to share their mission with us. We arranged to meet with Pumy, one of their "professional witnesses", after the presentation. In a dimly lit room surrounded by supplies for the HIV/AIDS Task Force Pumy tells us why she does what she does.

"It was my wish that one day I would get a job that would help me serve the people, sick people—I hoped that one day I could be involved in helping others by getting involved with the Luke Commission."

Pumy has a passion for helping other people. She also has four children. Pumy is a widow and she is HIV positive. "I talk to my children about my job, but I have not yet told them that I am HIV. Some of them are still young and they might get scared. They hear stories out there about HIV. I do not want them to be frightened, so I am protecting them until they are a little older."

Working several days a week for the Commission, she believes that her HIV status helps the people she serves because they can identify with her. Her clients do not believe that she is HIV positive. "Sometimes I will just show them my medicine so that they will believe me."

On any given day Pumy meets with individuals that are waiting to hear the results of their HIV test. "If I tell you the results and you start crying, I make sure that you don't leave my department upset. I want you to go with hope—with strength. I will not let anyone leave without hope. My hope is that maybe God one day will bring a cure for the HIV. If the cure doesn't come, I am OK with that. I have an eternal life; my spiritual life is well even if my body is not."

"If the cure doesn't come, I am OK with that. I have an eternal life; my spiritual life is well even if my body is not."

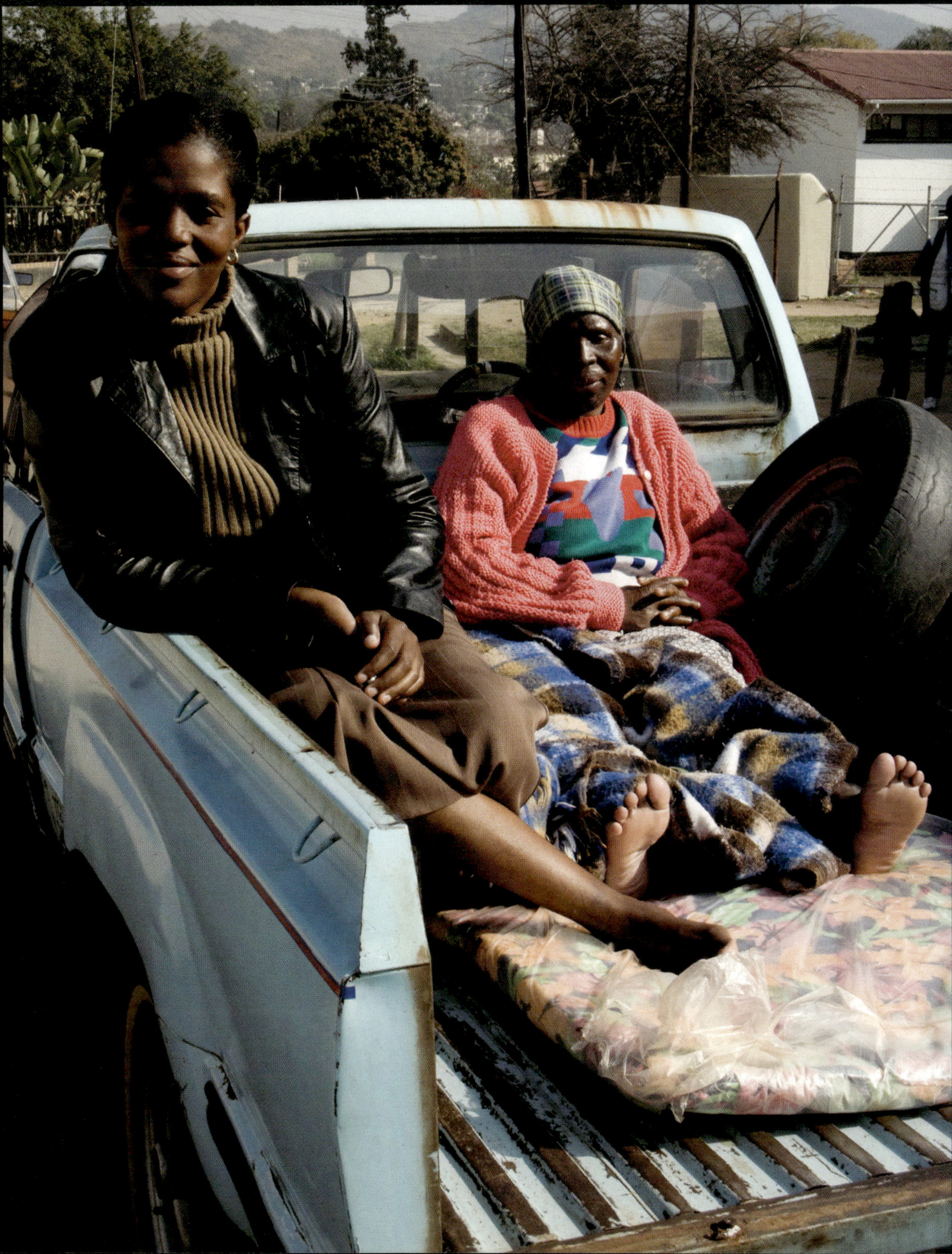

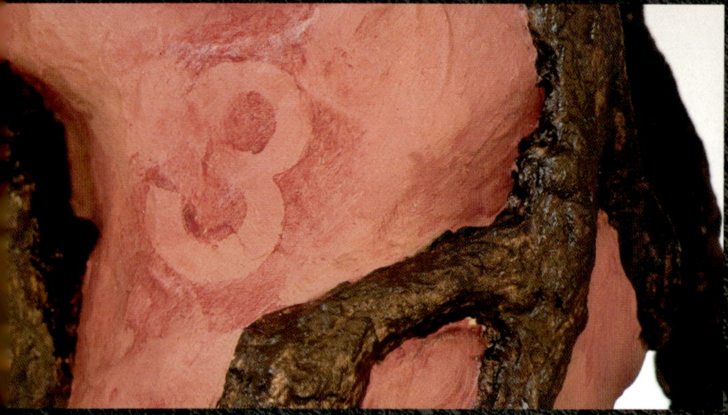
3
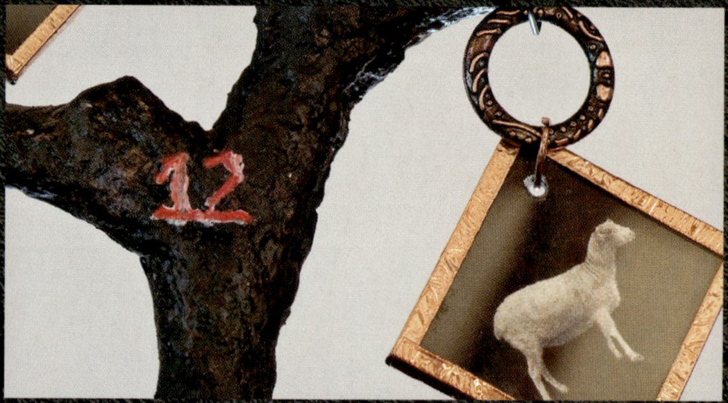
12

"Although the world is full of suffering, it is full also of the overcoming of it."

—HELEN KELLER

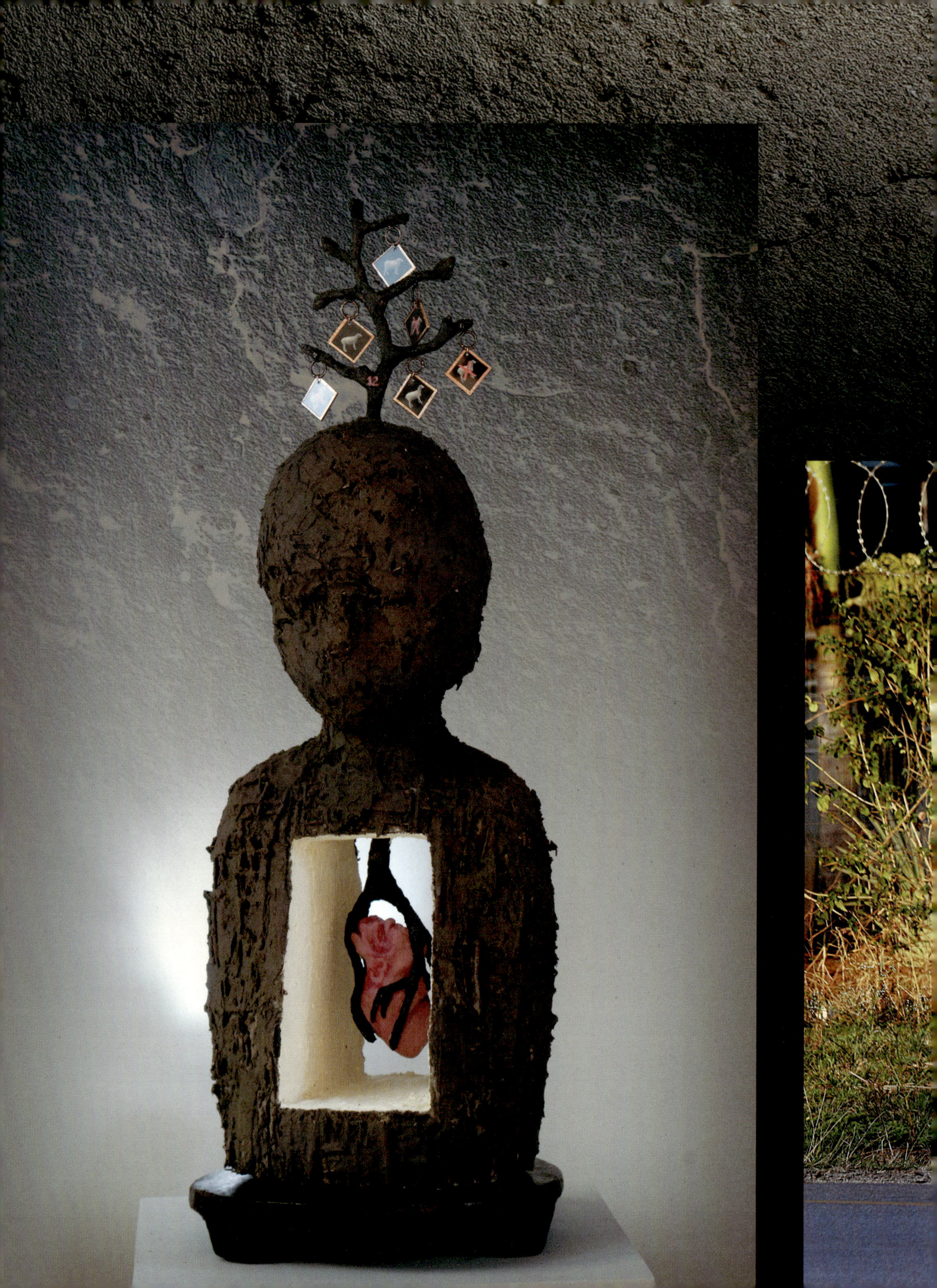

I AM WATTLE AND DAUB, A WITHERED TREE, A HOLLOW HOUSE. THE BLIGHT MARKS MY LAMBS AND BRUISES MY PREMATURE FRUIT. THE ANCESTORS CALL DOWN, "WHAT CURSE HAS SEIZED THE HARVEST OF OUR ANCIENT SEED?" IN THE STILL OF THE EMPTY, THE HEART OF ALPHA OMEGA BEATS A REQUIEM AND THE VIOLATED CORNERS OF THIS PRECARIOUS DWELLING CRY OUT FROM BEFORE TIME.

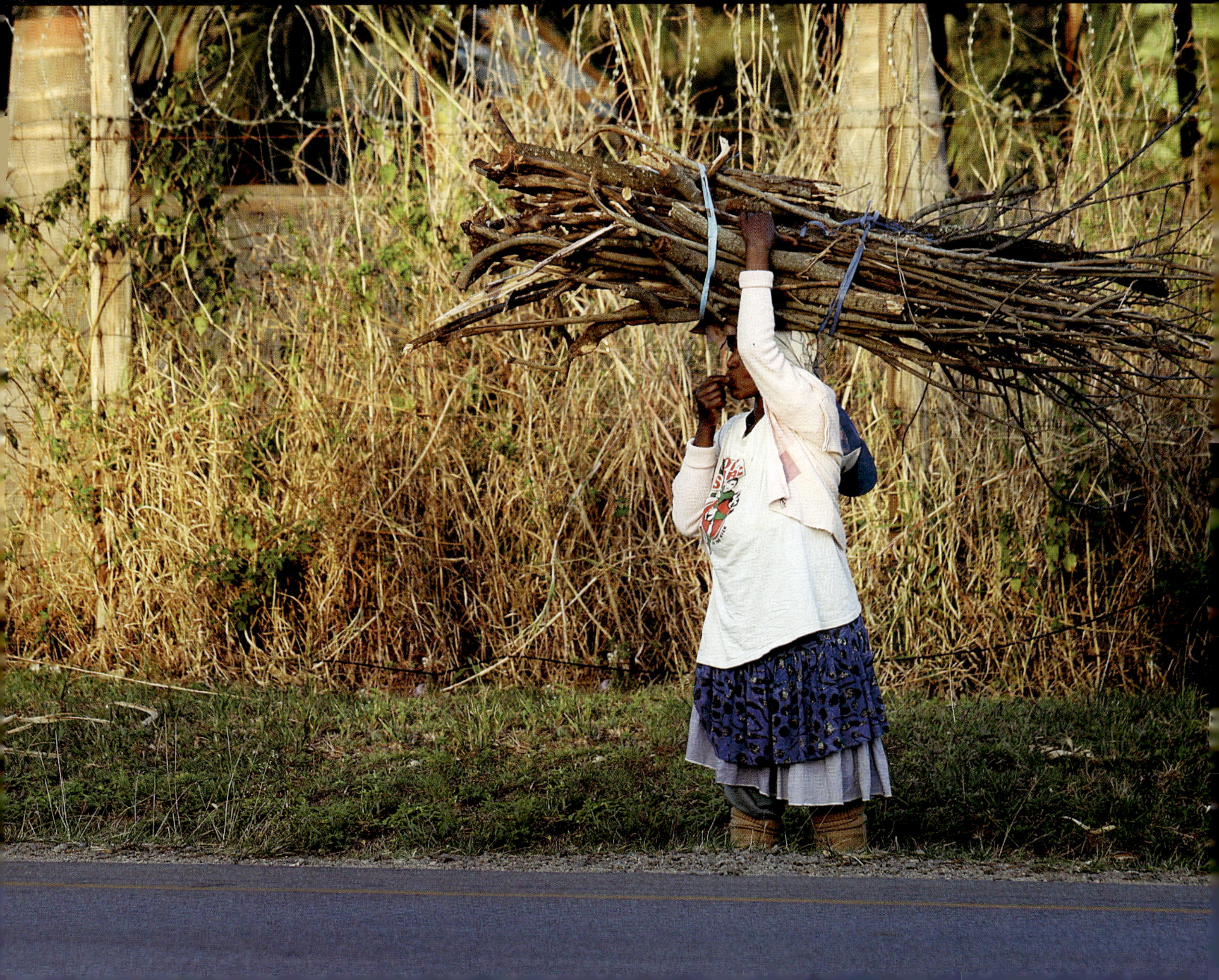

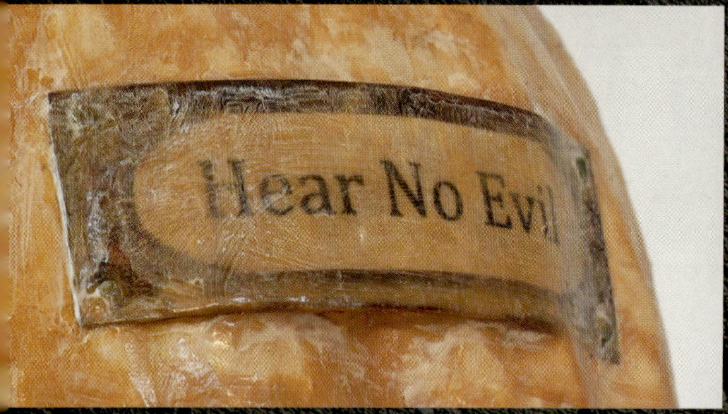
Hear No Evil

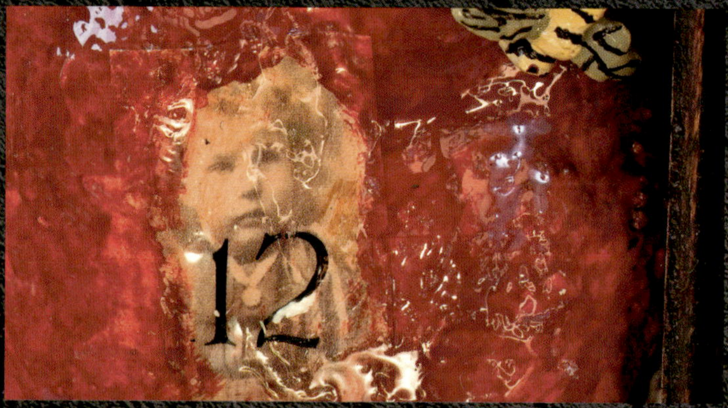
12

"By far the most dangerous foe we have to fight is apathy—indifference from whatever cause, not from a lack of knowledge, but from carelessness, from absorption in other pursuits, from a contempt bred of self satisfaction."

—WILLIAM OSLER

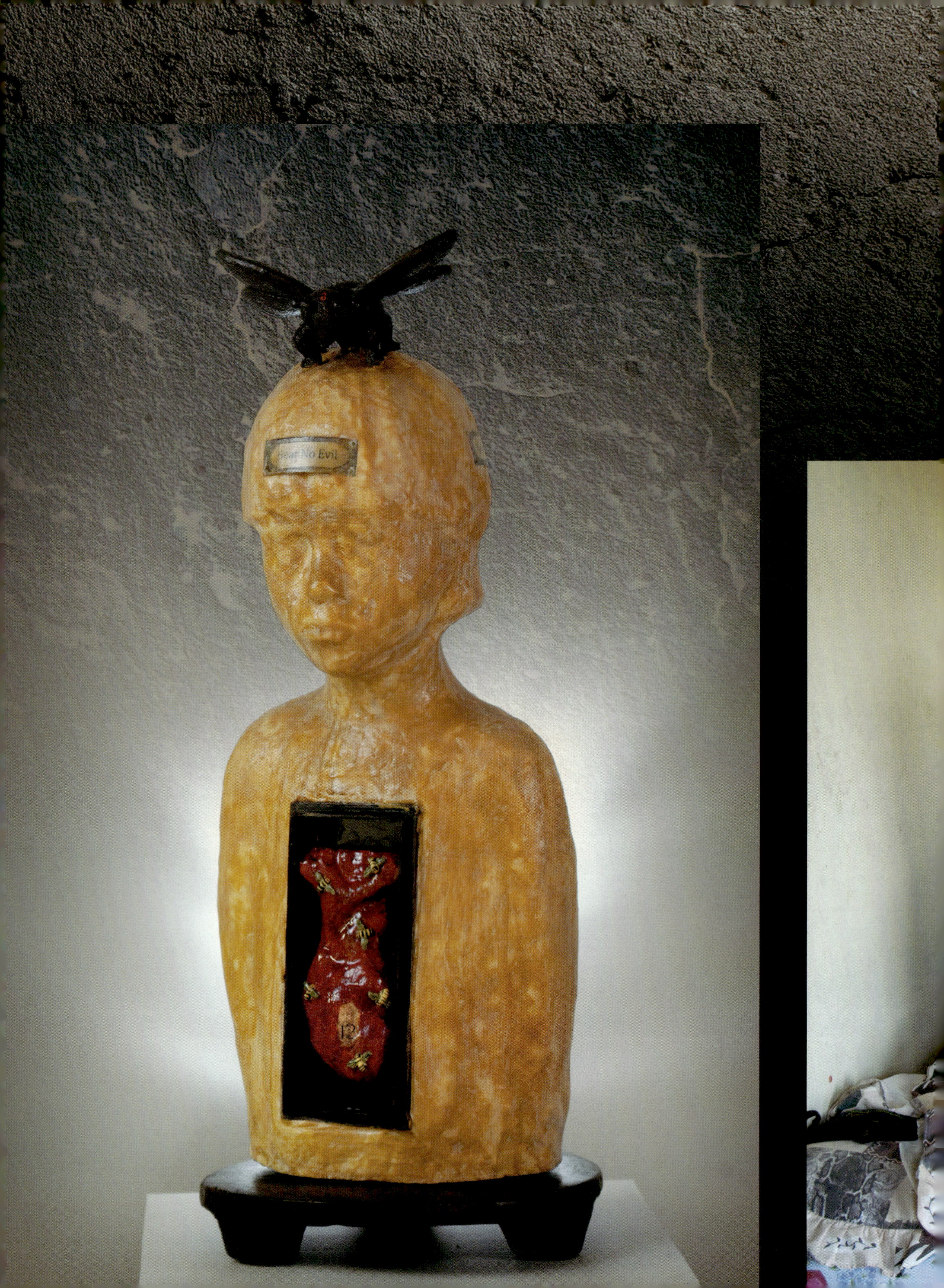
Hear No Evil

I AM SEALED IN THE WAX OF APATHY. THE STING OF NEGLECT WOULD POISON MY HEART, CRUEL ANESTHESIA TO THE FEELINGS OF CHANGE. BRING YOUR SELFLESS CANDLE, YOUR FLAME OF COMPASSION. EVER SO SMALL, IT BURNS THE FLAME OF DELIVERANCE. FEAR NOT THE SWEAT OF HUMAN FLESH, THE STENCH OF RELATIONSHIP. THE BALM OF RESTORATION WILL FIND ITSELF IN SOOTY HANDS SINGED BY EMPATHY'S FLAME.

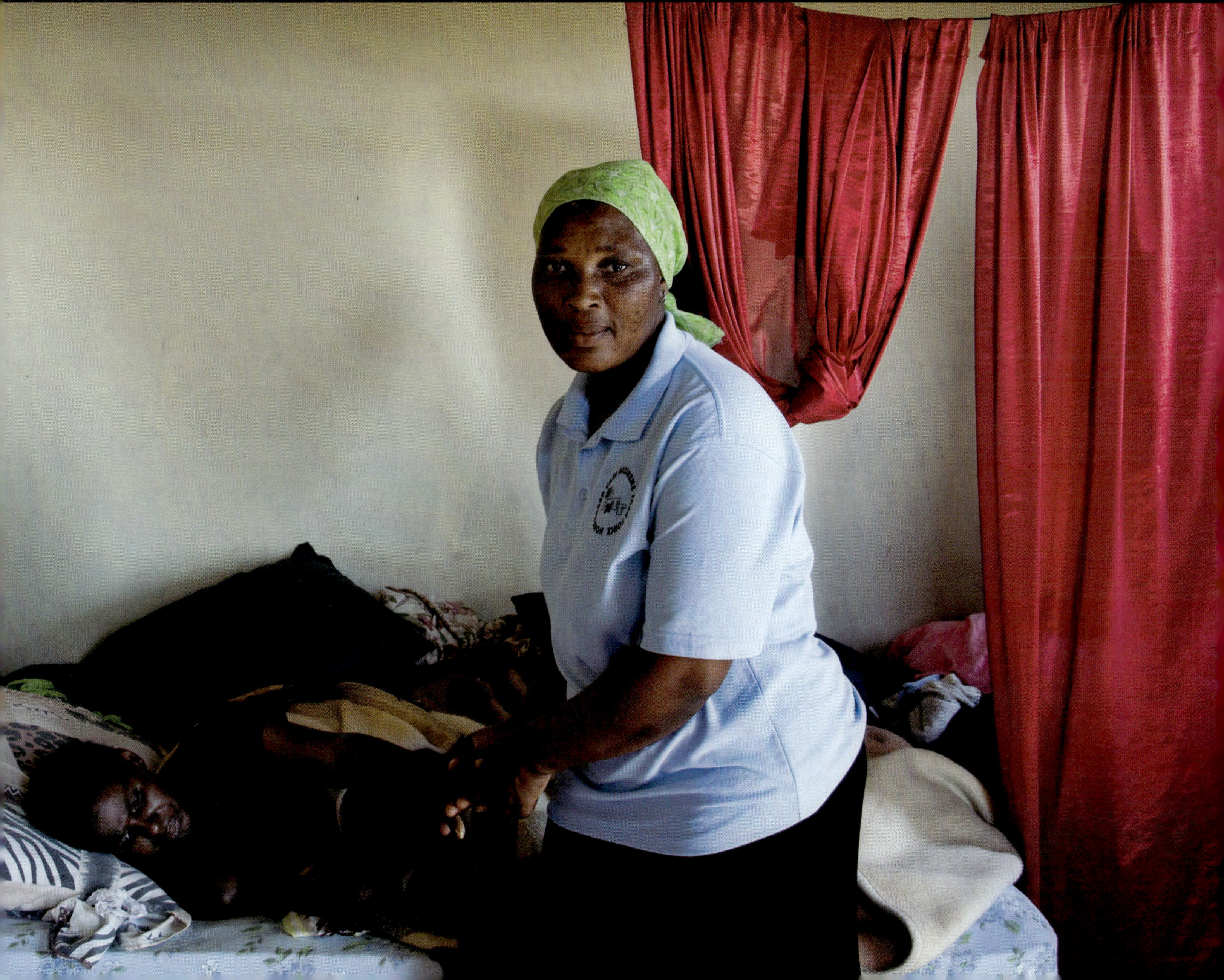

THE NURSES

She is a trained nurse working every day in the throes of the plague. Getting out of Swaziland and going back to school has its appeal. A re-entry into academia would be a justifiable ticket out, but she won't leave. She loves her people.

During our brief visit she requests that she remain anonymous. As we begin to talk we understand this request. We are stunned at her openness; something akin to our American feminist archetype.

"The way this country is now... well, nurses are tired. There are so many things that relate to HIV that are coming in. People are getting sick in so many different ways that you don't know how to manage them. There is a lot to do. There is a lot to take care of and there is a lot you have to see. So the nurses are always getting burnt out. People here don't know how to get it all out—how to deal with the grief."

She continues.

"Can I say that so many nurses are dying from HIV because of the business of them not taking care of themselves? You prick yourself. Okay, we get pricked every night and we end up not taking it seriously. We just say, 'I'll do it,' (although we are exhausted) and we postpone taking care of ourselves. I delivered a baby in an emergency and didn't wear gloves. I was thinking at this point, I have likely already been exposed. You give so much and just get tired. You get drained. It's a matter of going on to do what needs to be done."

"I don't know why I still smile because there's really nothing to smile about. I still pray every day and if I know that I done all I can do then there is nothing more I can do. If I could do more, I would see that at the end of the day someone would be there to take care of the nurses... emotionally."

"People here don't know how to get it all out—how to deal with the grief."

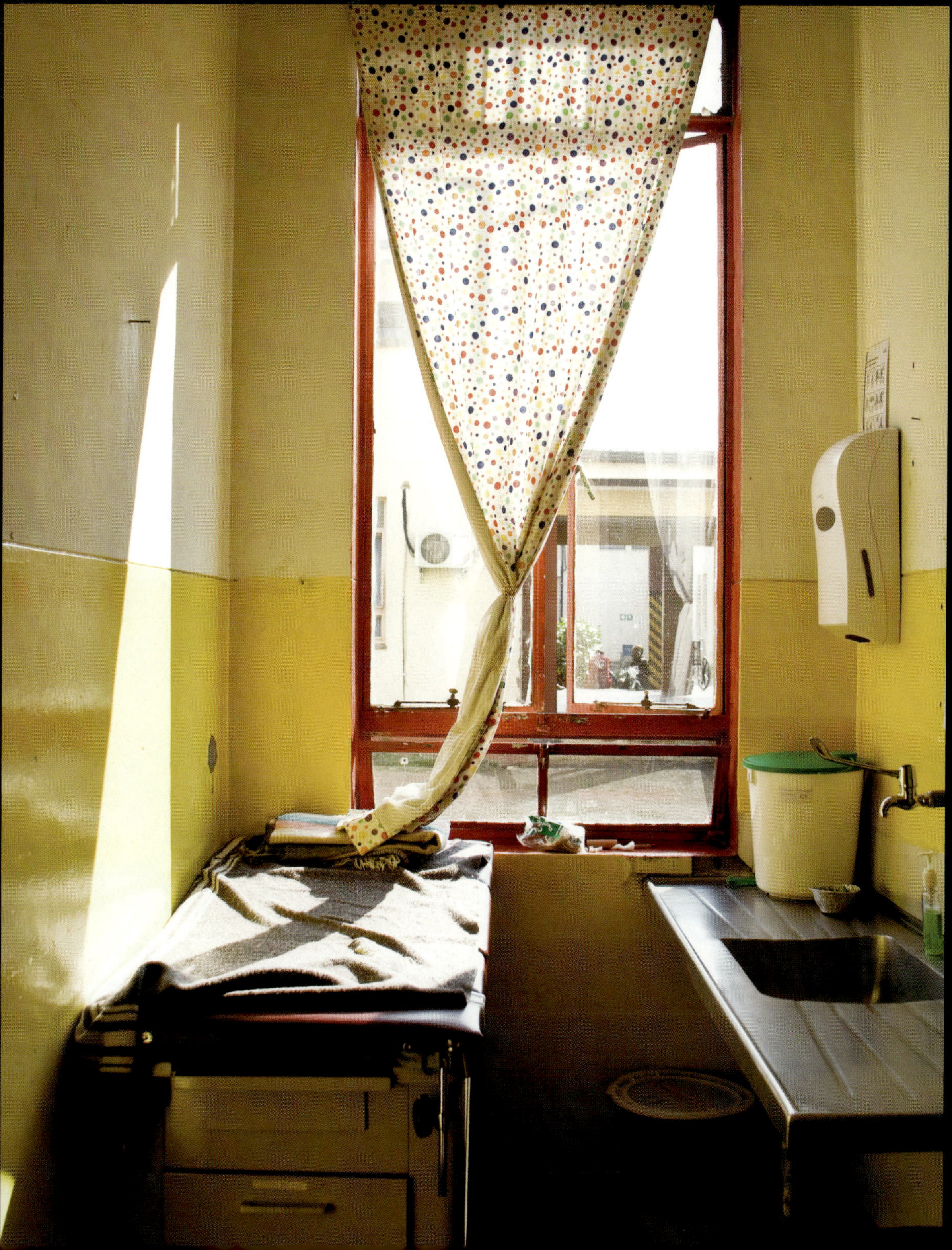

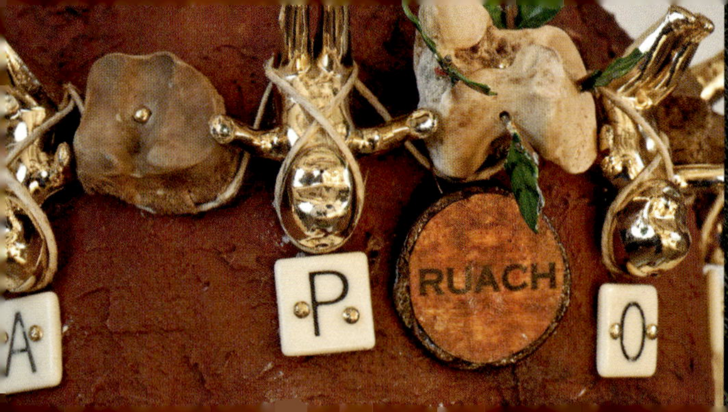
A
P
RUACH
O

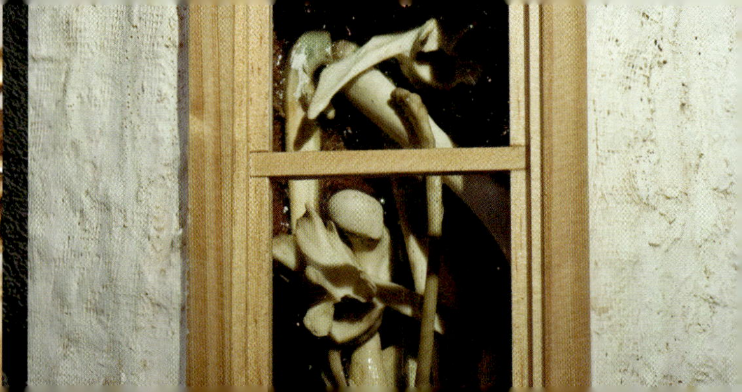

"There are people in the world so hungry, that God cannot appear to them except in the form of bread."

—MOHANDAS K. GANDHI

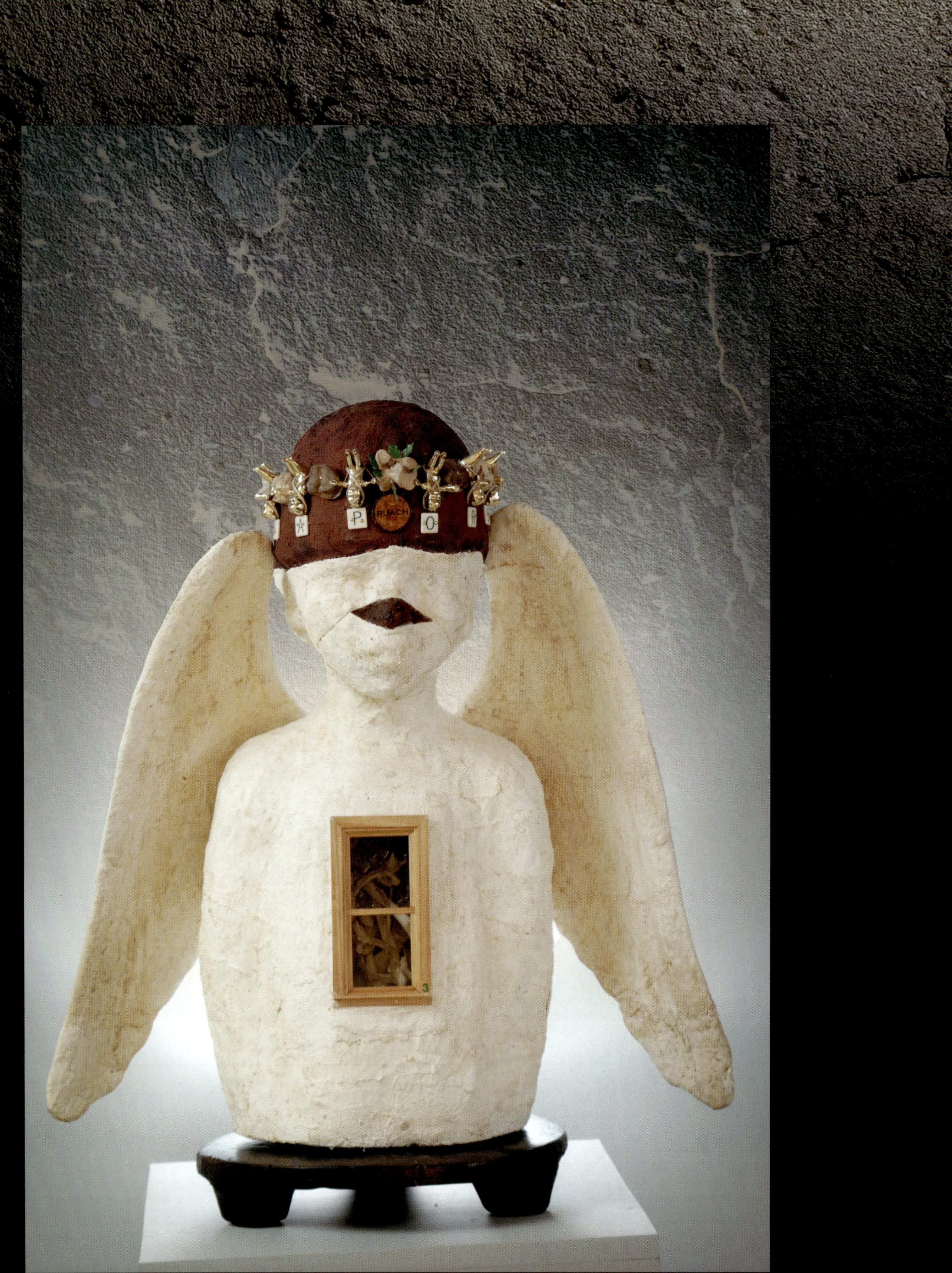

A
P
RUACH
O
3

I AM SCORCHED EARTH AND DRY BONES. MY TENDER SPROUTS HAVE WITHERED—PARCHED TONGUES, EMPTY BELLIES. DEATH VISITS MY DOOR TO DECREE THAT SHADOWY SENTINELS WILL GUARD THE WINDOW OF MY SOUL. MEMENTO MORI ARE MY CHILDREN NOW, DANCING IN THE CORNERS OF MY MEMORY, CATCHING THE LIGHT OF MY TEARS.

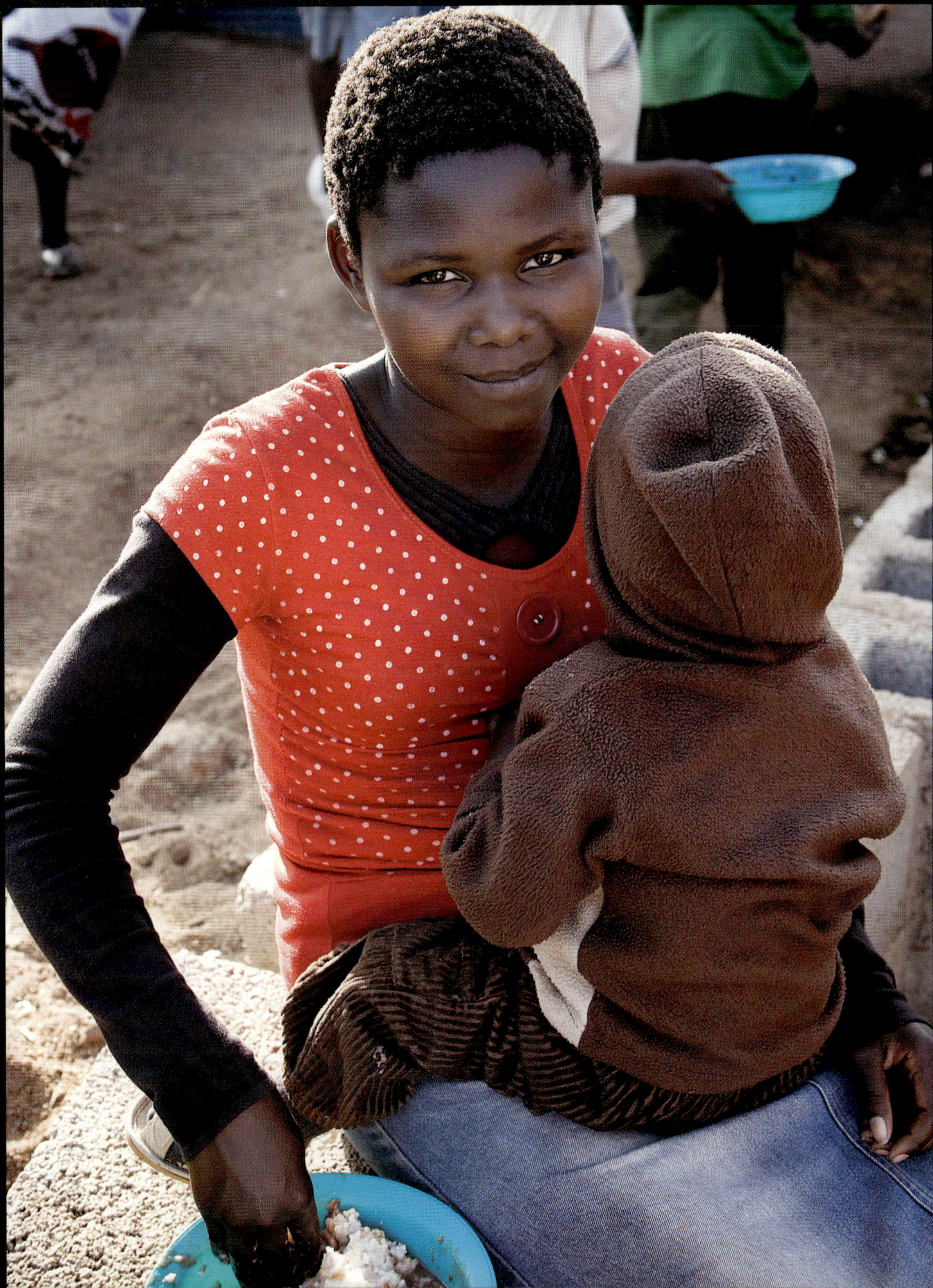

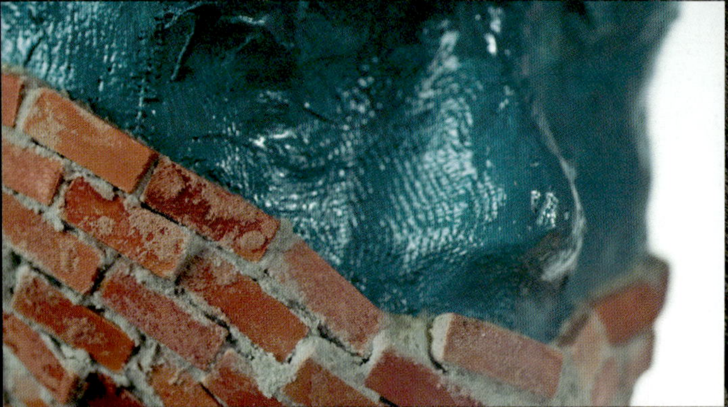

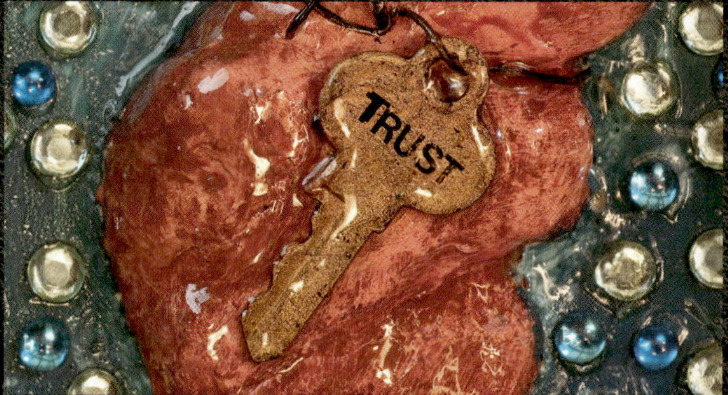
TRUST

"We who lived in concentration camps can remember the men who walked through the huts comforting others, giving away their last piece of bread. They may have been few in number, but they offer sufficient proof that everything can be taken from a man but one thing: the last of human freedoms—to choose one's attitude in any given set of circumstances—to choose one's own way."

—VIKTOR FRANKL

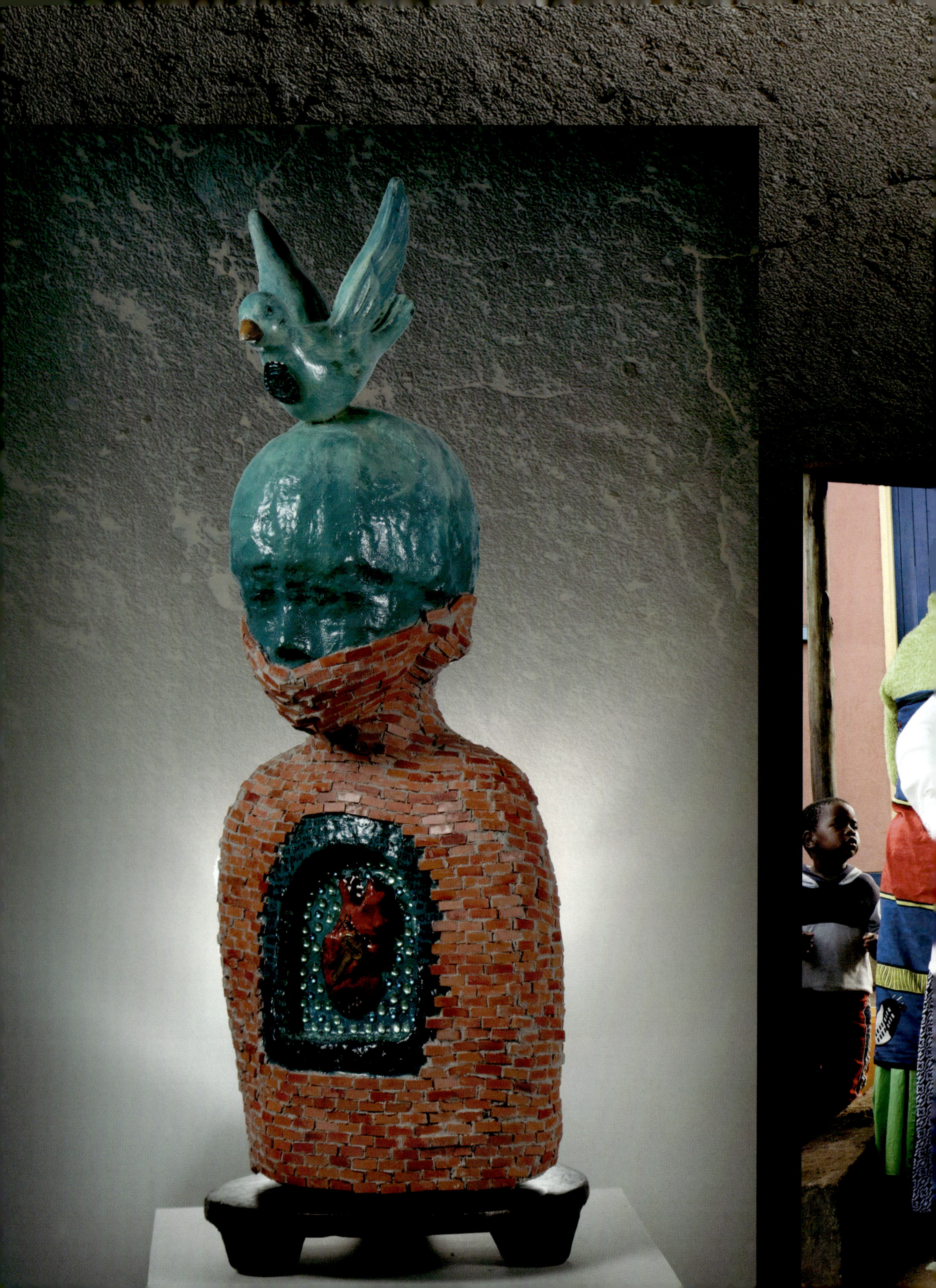

I AM BRICKS AND BLUE. I AM DUALITY. JOY WILL REST ON ME EVEN WHILE I AM BOUND BY WALLS OF CIRCUMSTANCE. MY SISTER WILL LIE DOWN WITH ME AND SOOTHE MY WOUNDS WITH EMPATHY. I AM NOT ALONE. I LIE DOWN IN DARKNESS COVERED IN PEACE. THE PULSE OF MY HEART AGAINST THIS FORTRESS BRUISES ME, BUT IT WILL NOT YIELD THE LOVE OF COMMUNITY. TRUST UNLOCKS THE SECRETS OF MY INTERNAL PARADISE.

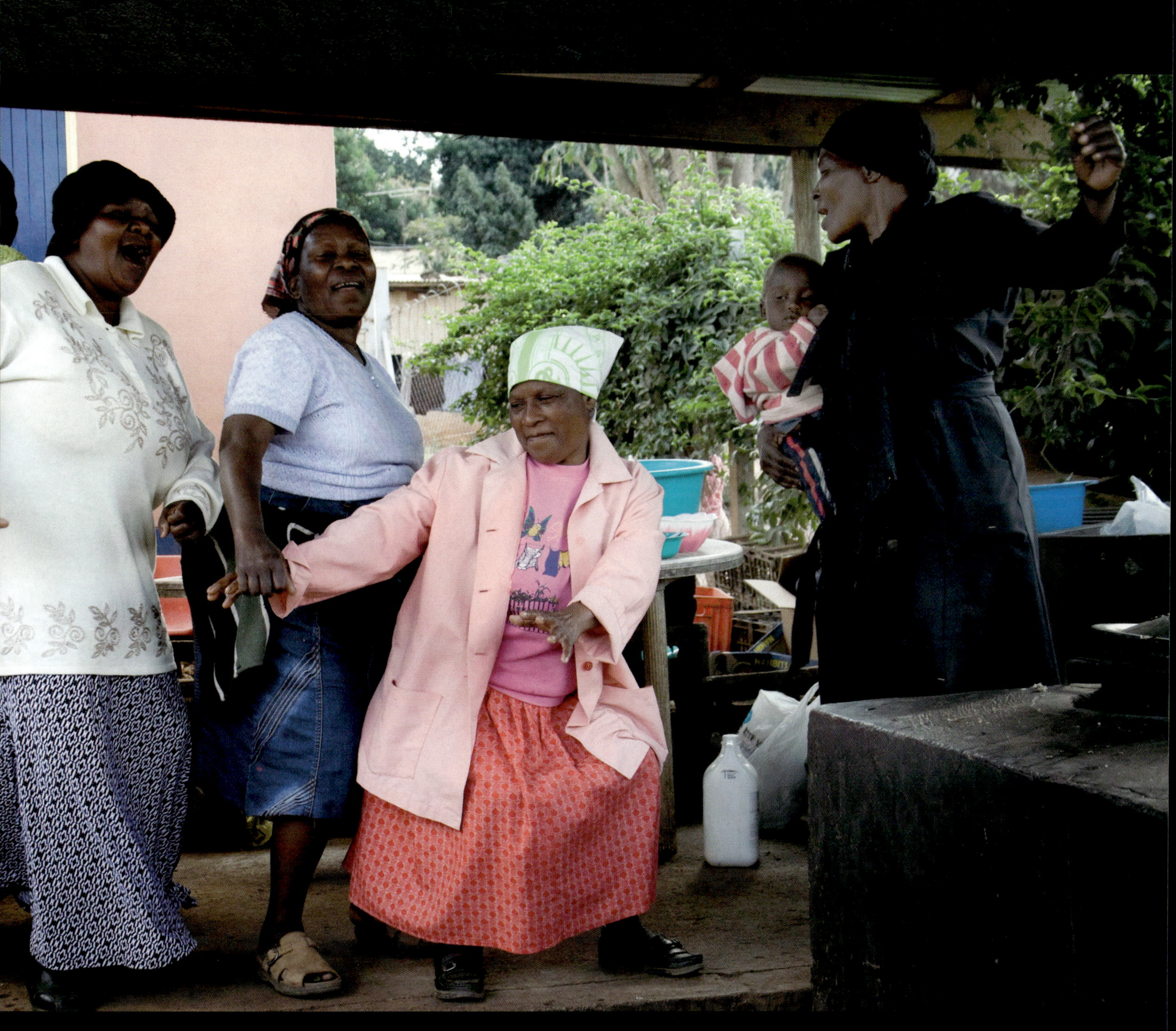

EVELYN'S STORY

Evelyn didn't impress me as someone who tired easily. Her robust character and apparently endless energy are in stark contrast to the world she enters every day. Traveling often alone in her car, she frequents some of the most remote and disease-ridden areas in Swaziland. By all accounts she is a traveling hospice nurse. Acquainted with death and dying, she is armed with grace. Evelyn and her dear friend Mary are the co-founders of the HIV / AIDS Task Force. They are the Sister Theresa's of Swaziland. Compassion feeds their efforts every day compelling them into the unknown with a fearlessness that exceeds comprehension.

As we traveled with Evelyn on this day, the extreme adverse conditions we confronted were shocking. We drove into areas carved by deep clay canyons and framed by dense outcroppings of thick bush. Tucked between untamed rolling hills and rocky ledges were small dirt floored huts and one-roomed cinder block houses, each sheltering the desperately sick. At each location Evelyn was welcomed with joy. She took the hand of the patient, spoke words of comfort, offered nursing care, food and provisions. Before leaving she prayed and then she sang. Some struggled to sit just so they could sing along with her. Several times, as we were leaving, one stop after another, Evelyn turned to us, shook her head and whispered, "She will die soon," or "He won't be here next time," and "The children will be orphaned."

I was struck by a sense of hopelessness. So I asked her, "Evelyn, have you ever encountered a situation that was too much to bear? How did you deal with it?"

Evelyn lifted her eyes and contemplated this question, "You know, my greatest joy is when I can help someone physically, emotionally, and spiritually. But, I do remember one time that was most difficult."

"I remember visiting a woman that had been raped and mutilated. She was not accepted at the hospital in Johannesburg so they sent her back to Swaziland. Her relatives blamed her, saying she brought the rape on herself. They let her come back home, but forced her to stay in a small room separate from the rest of her family. She was not to be touched. We found her with a glass with very little water in it and sand. She had this because she had nothing to eat. She was drinking water with sand. We went every day and bathed her sores, gave her food, gave her medicine, washed her clothes, and cared for her. No one would go to her. We went to her for three weeks every day even when the relatives were all there, because they would not touch her. It was so stressful. Every day before we would leave, Mary and I would sit down in the office and pray, talk, and cry together. But I was happy in the end. We helped her for three weeks and even though she died, she was healed in her mind, because she knew we would be there for her every day and she was not alone."

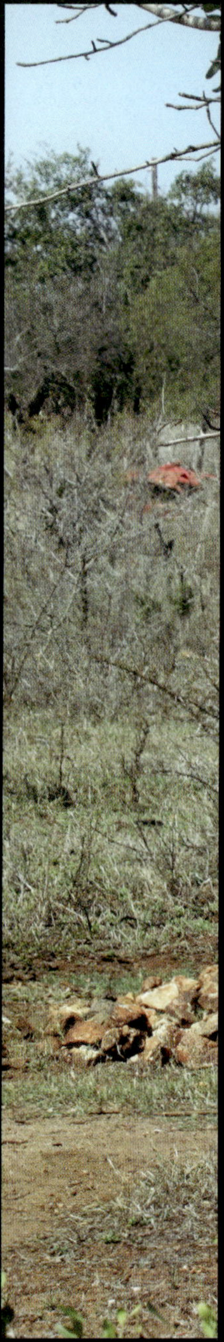

"Several times, as we were leaving, one stop after another, Evelyn turned to us, shook her head and whispered, 'She will die soon,' or 'He won't be here next time.'"

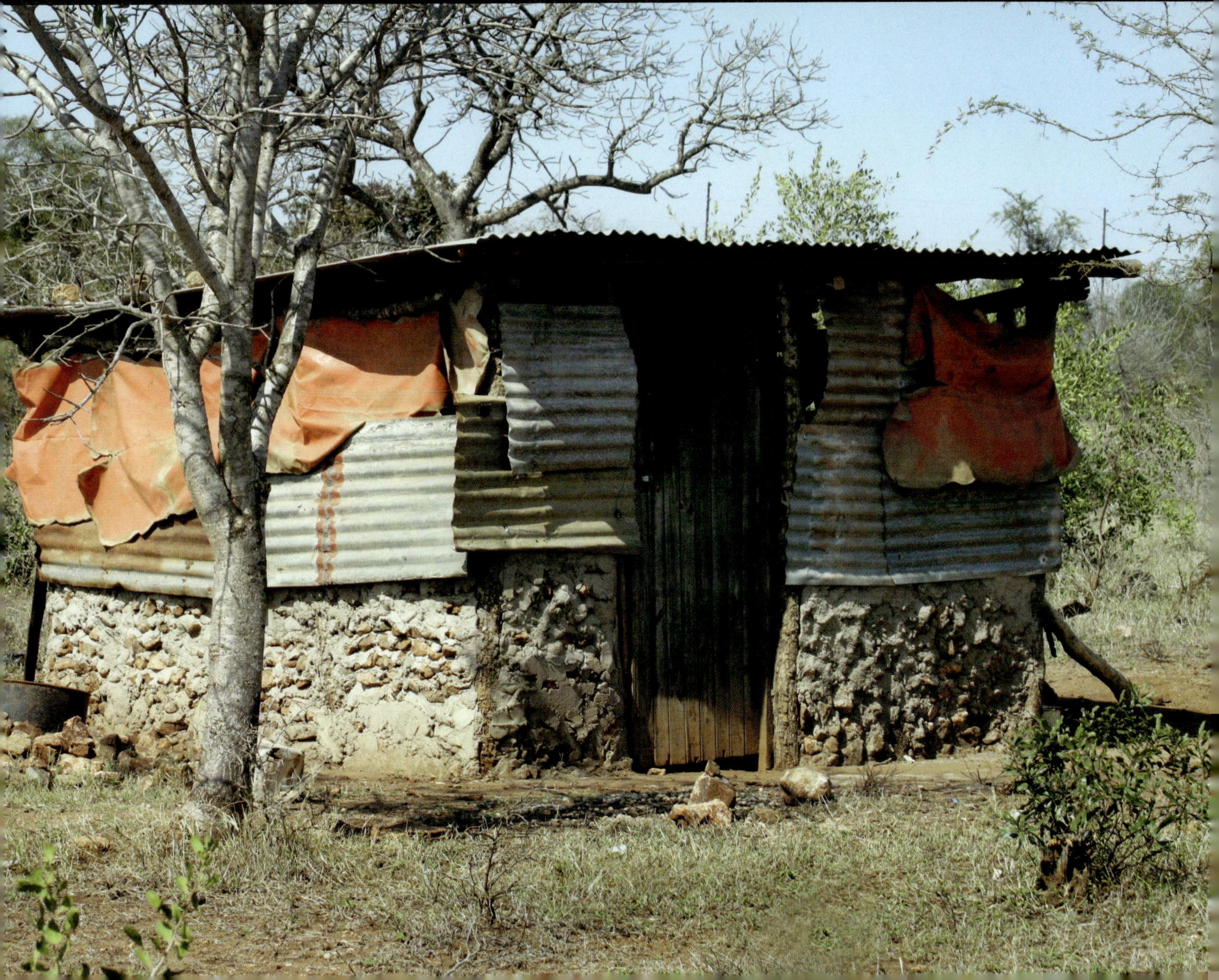

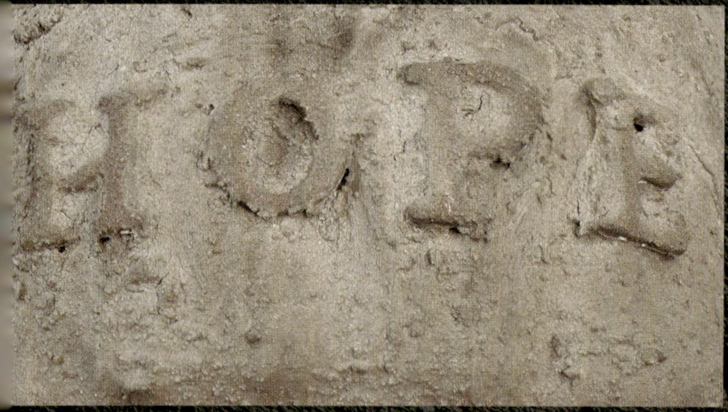
HOPE

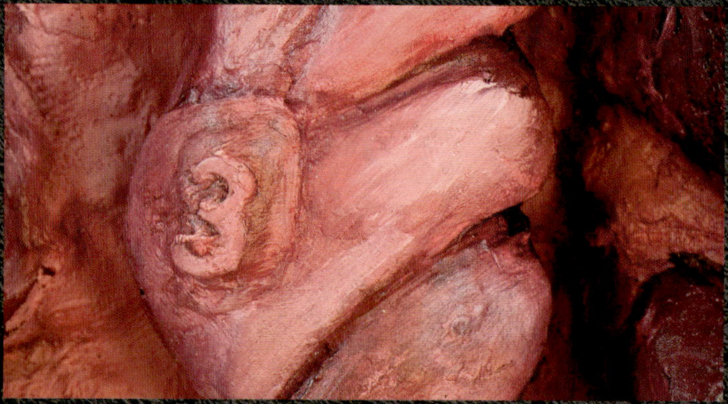
3

"Do not depend on the hope of results. You may have to face the fact that your work will be apparently worthless and even achieve no result at all, if not perhaps results opposite to what you expect. As you get used to this idea, you start more and more to concentrate not on the results, but on the value, the rightness, the truth of the work itself. You gradually struggle less and less for an idea and more and more for specific people. In the end, it is the reality of personal relationship that saves everything."

—THOMAS MERTON

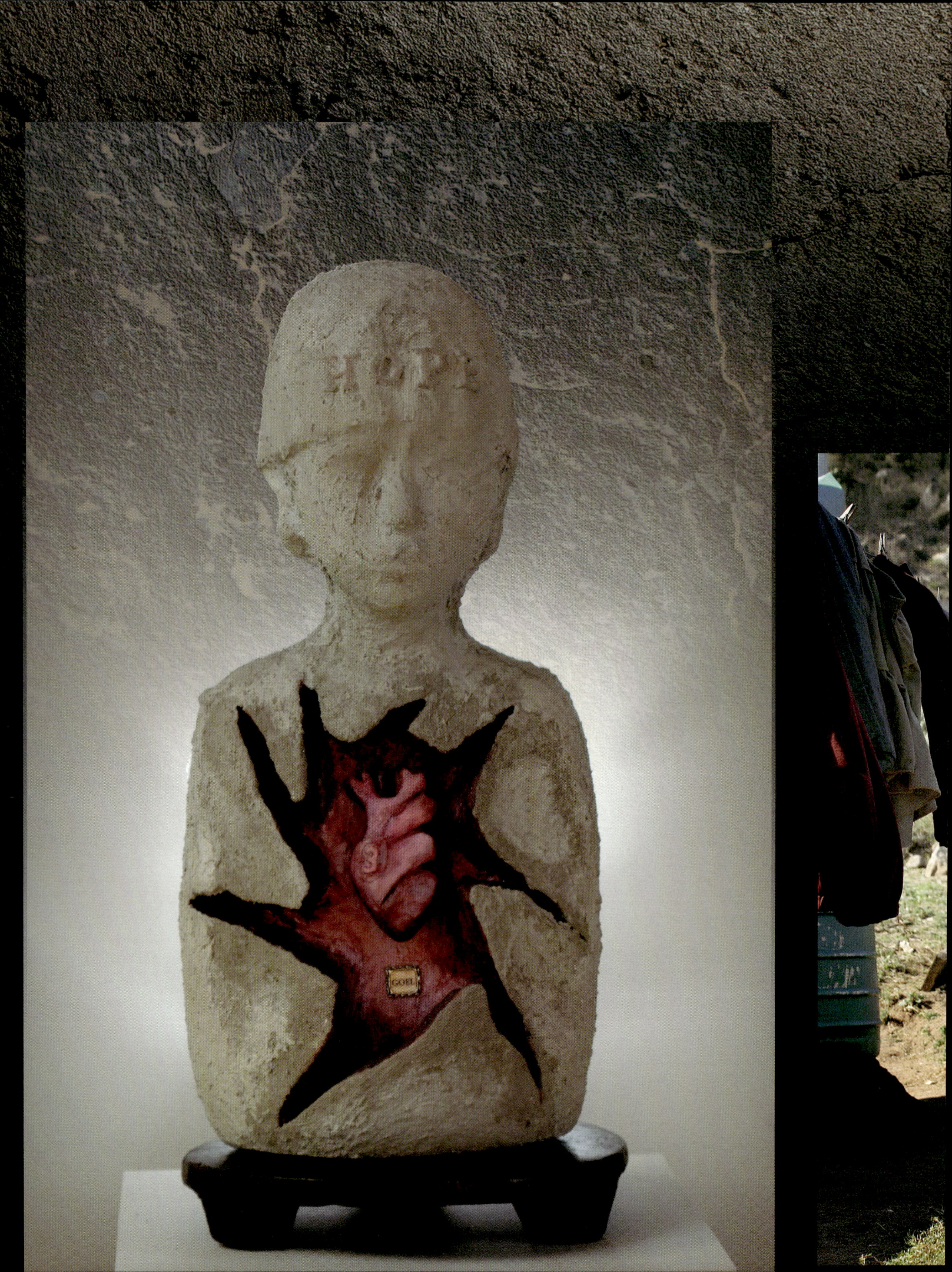
HOPE
GOEL

I AM COVERED IN THE CEMENT OF BURDEN. FROZEN ARE THE DREAMS OF MY FUTURE. WHO WOULD TEACH ME OF GOEL? THE POWER OF A FREED SOUL TO RENDER LIFE AGAIN, A SONG OF THE AGES, I WOULD KNOW. CALL OUT TO ME FROM DEPTHS WITHIN AND BREAK THIS CAST OF NO TOMORROW.

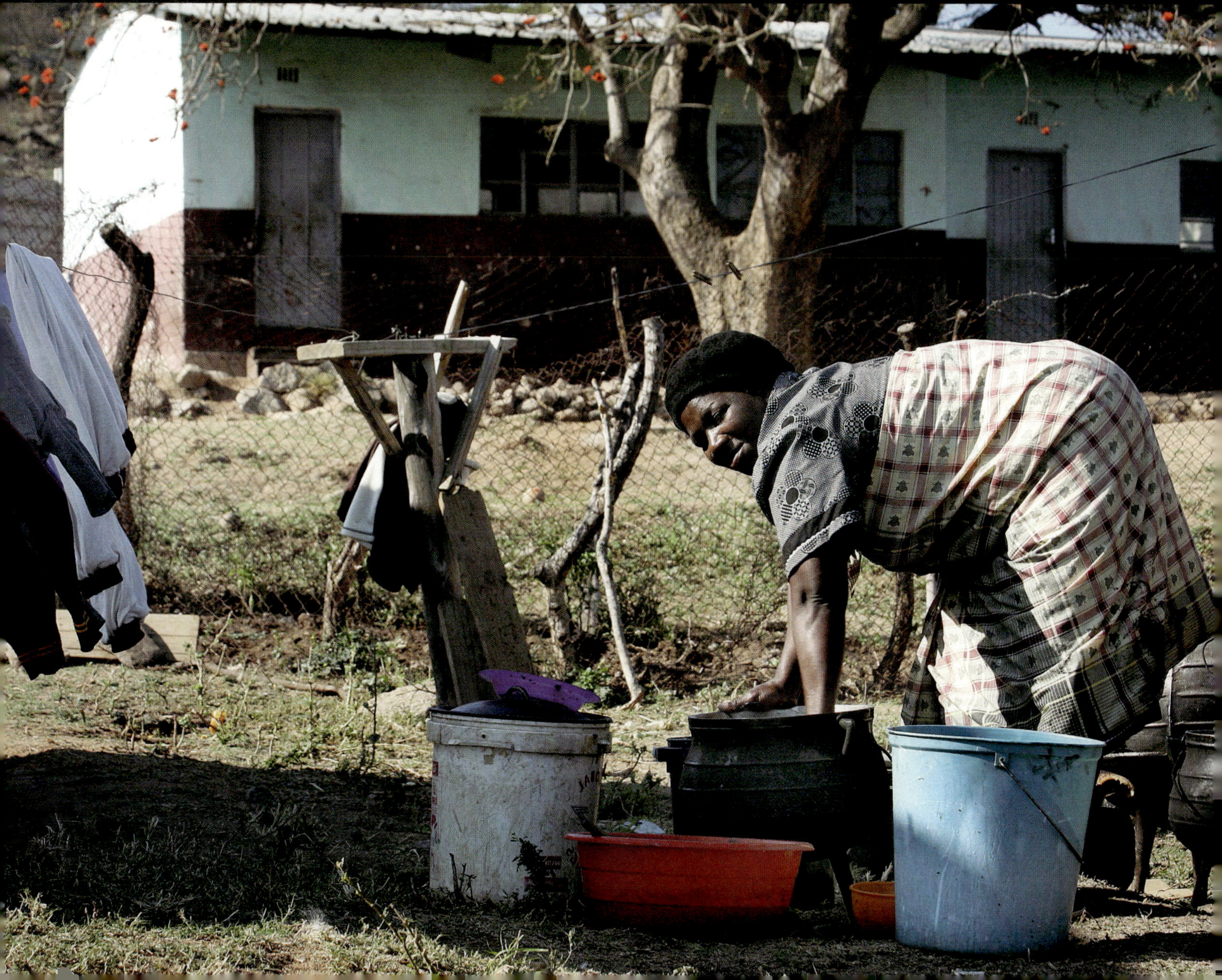

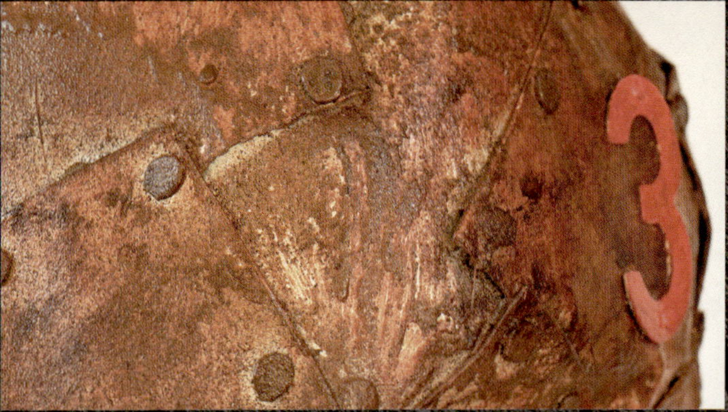
3

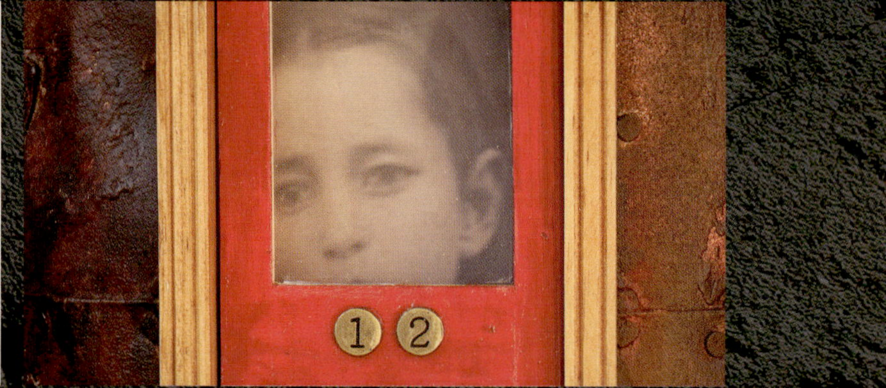
1 2

"I have learned two lessons in my life: first, there are no sufficient literary, psychological, or historical answers to human tragedy, only moral ones. Second, just as despair can come to one another only from other human beings, hope, too, can be given to one only by other human beings."

—ELIE WIESEL

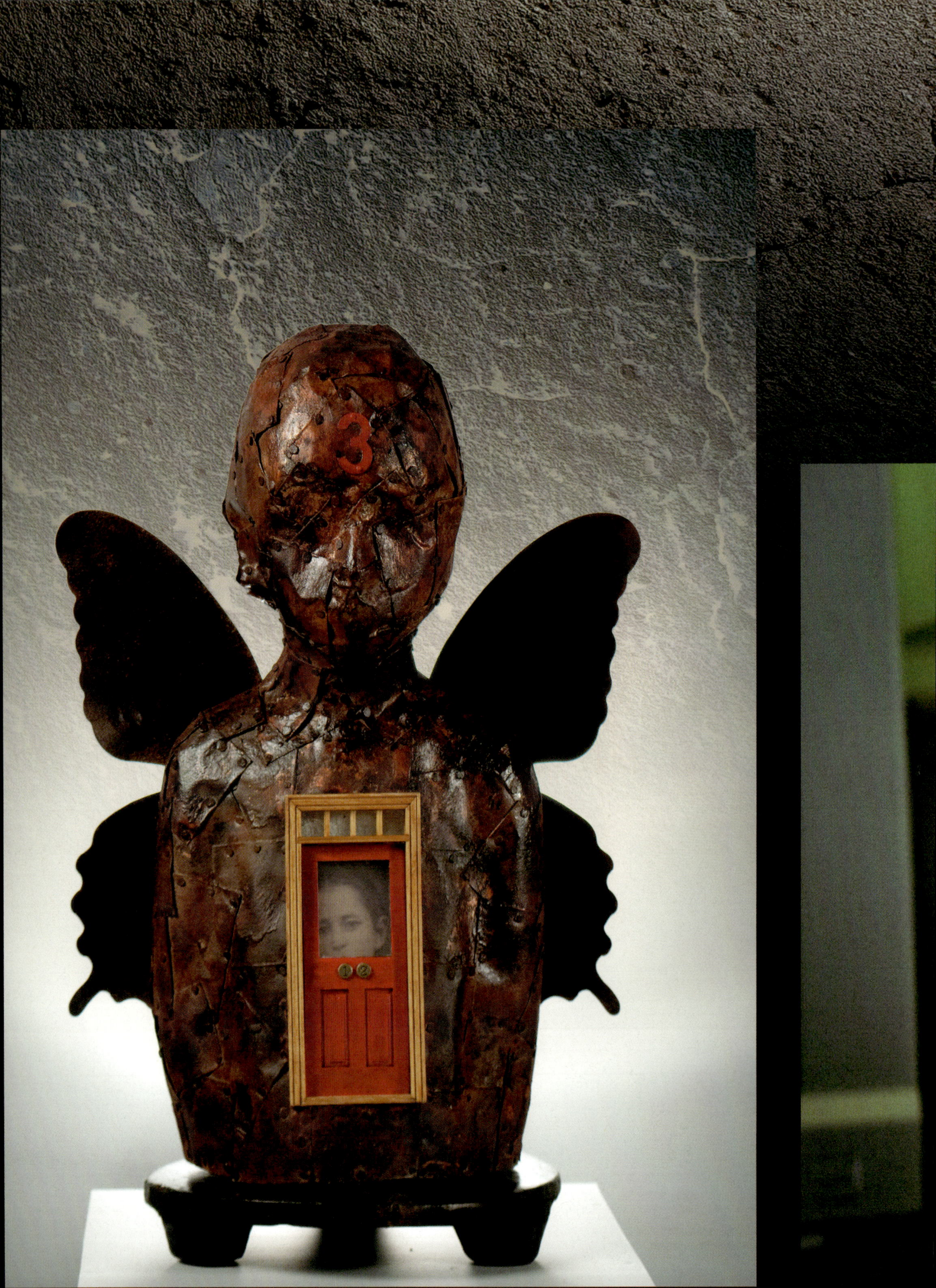

I AM A CLOSED DOOR. BEHIND THE DOOR OF MY HEART I DWELL. I HAVE FASHIONED THIS PLACE FOR MYSELF; A ROOM FROM WHICH I WATCH THE WORLD. ARROWS OF INDIFFERENCE HAVE SHAPED MY ARMOR. FLESH TO RUST; I CARRY THE FOSSIL WINGS OF MY DREAMS, WEIGHTED AND USELESS, YEARNING FLIGHT.

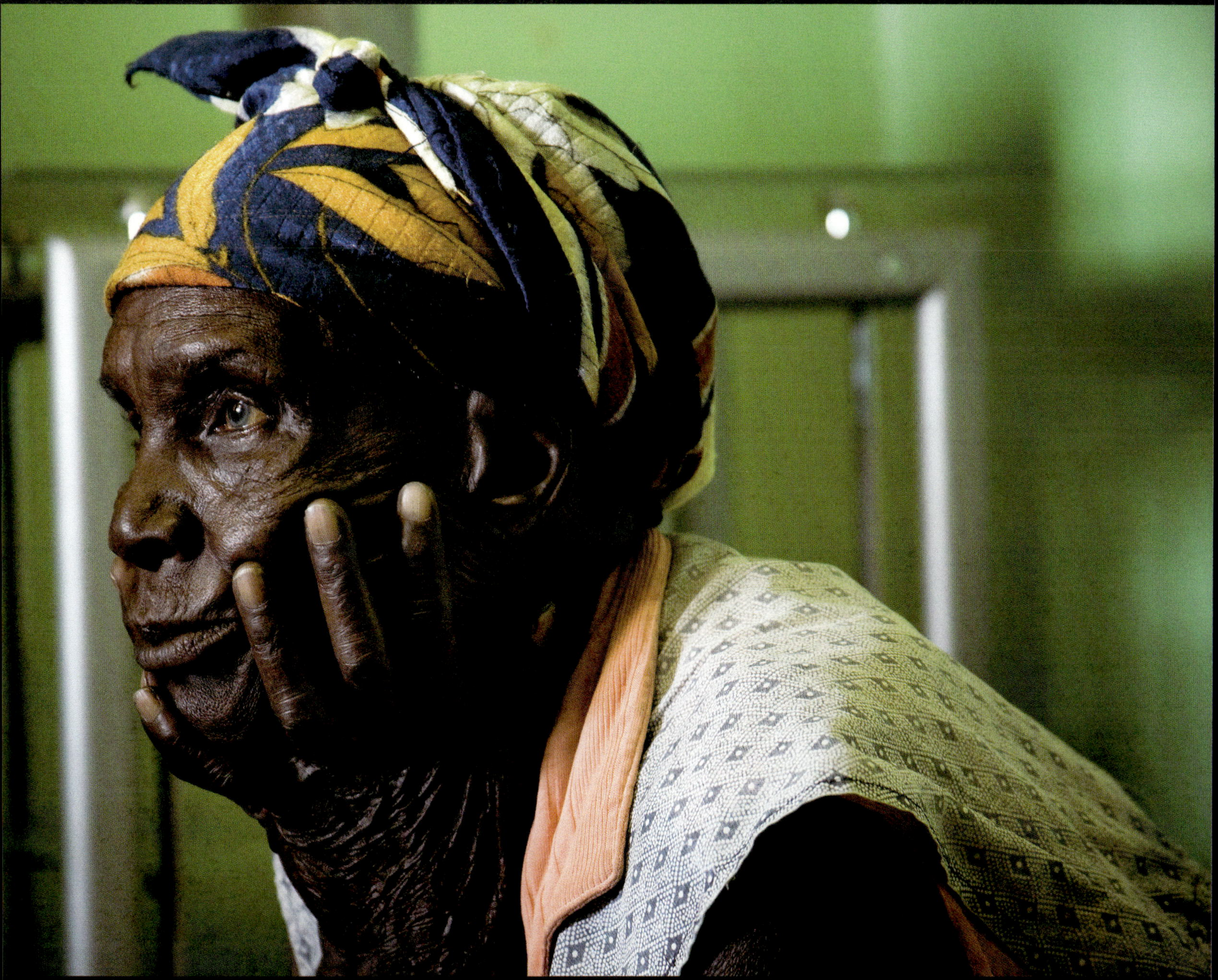

PATIENCE'S STORY

Patience has a smile that is among the most beautiful I have ever seen. This could only be trumped by her absolutely infectious giggle. The mid-morning sun in Bhalekane sparkles off her dark skin and dances in her eyes. She moves quickly in the gathering heat of the day, skillfully coordinating volunteers. True to her name, she patiently sets up stations, collecting resources and organizing the free clinic where hundreds will receive assistance. Patience is the Head Nurse at the Bhalekane Nazarene Clinic. Although her radiant smile would imply otherwise, she has seen her share of suffering.

Patience recalls the story of a young boy who was treated at the clinic.

"An eight-year-old was brought to the clinic by his Go-Go. He was very sick with Tuberculosis (TB). His parents had died from AIDS, so I ordered that he be tested for HIV. He tested positive. He would need to go to the hospital immediately to begin a regimen of Antiretroviral (ARV) drugs. But every time he came to the clinic he told the nurses that he couldn't go to the hospital because there was no money for transportation. So we did what we could, but his condition deteriorated because we are not equipped to initiate ARVs here."

His Go-Go was burdened with caring for other ill and needy family members. Her resources were very limited, so the clinic worked with local school children to take him back to his home after each treatment. This way he could rest at the clinic in a bed during the day.

"He was so sick. His lymph nodes were so swollen I had to open his mouth to feed him." Although his life depended on the care provided, his visits to the clinic were not consistent. Neither his Go-Go nor others in his dwindling family could manage the cost to get him to Bhalekane. In his condition, the 10K walk was just too much to bear. His visits became increasingly sporadic while his condition further deteriorated.

Patience relates how the nurses would hold tightly to his hand during his injections, because even the smallest of needles was too painful for his frail diseased body.

"His limbs became so inflamed and he couldn't eat anymore. It was so hard on him. If he could just get the ARV drugs he might have a chance. But he was so sick he could not go alone—such a tragedy. He needed to just stay and rest, but every day he had to go back and forth. I had to order that we stop the injections because he needed all his strength to rest. Everyone looked to us but we couldn't give him what he needed. Within two weeks from when we stopped giving the injections we were informed that the boy had died."

Unfortunately, this child's story is not unique. Patience and the staff at Bhalekane deal with cases like this every day.

"Patience, how do you deal with suffering every day?"

Through tears she responds, "We try, we try, but sometimes it is just so sad, so depressing. You don't feel the will to go on. You feel like you have failed everybody. But um, yeah you do, you do go on, (sigh). You pray every day—pray for the strength—because it is really hard. Sometimes we have problems of our own, but you feel like you've got this obligation, you know, about everything. For me, I will put myself aside. This is the calling that I have."

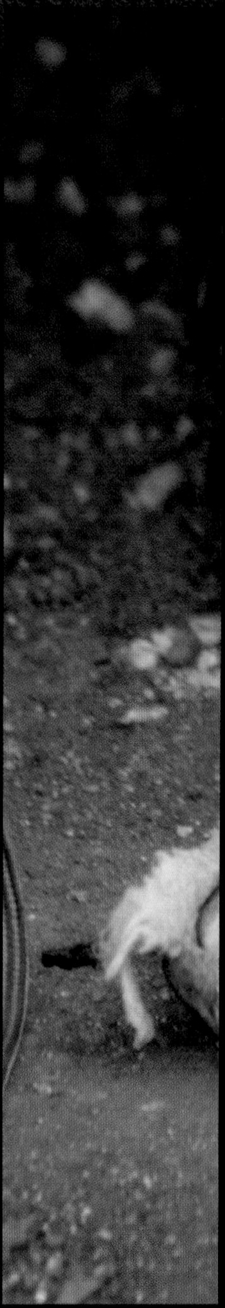

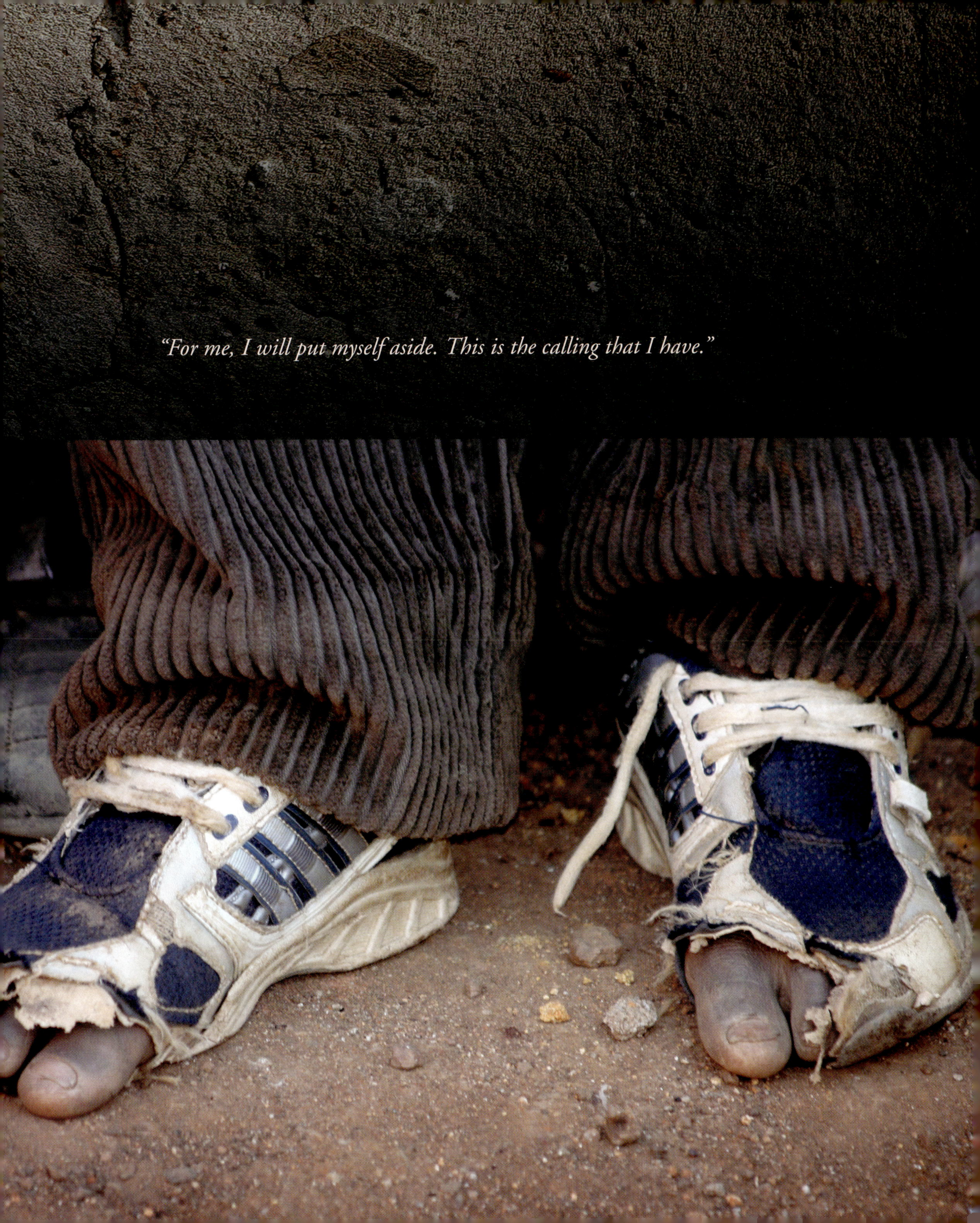
"For me, I will put myself aside. This is the calling that I have."

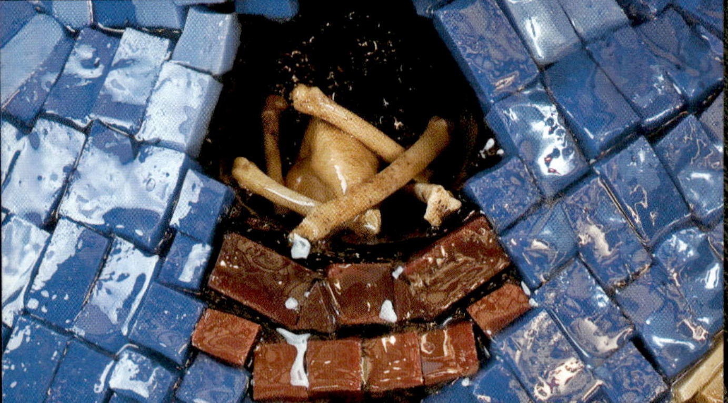
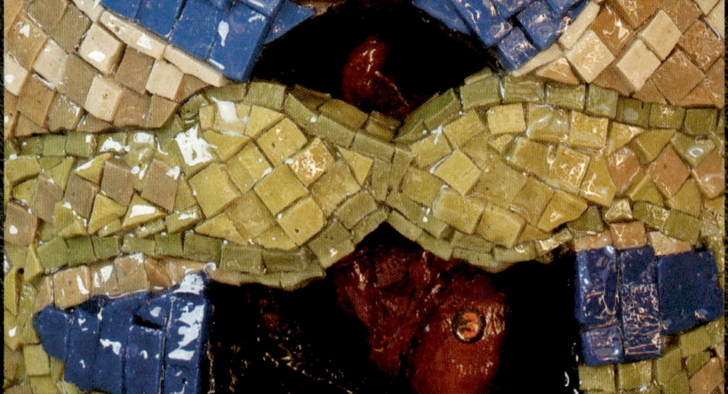

"There is no medicine like hope, no incentive so great, and no tonic so powerful as expectation of something better tomorrow."

—ORISON SWETT MARDEN

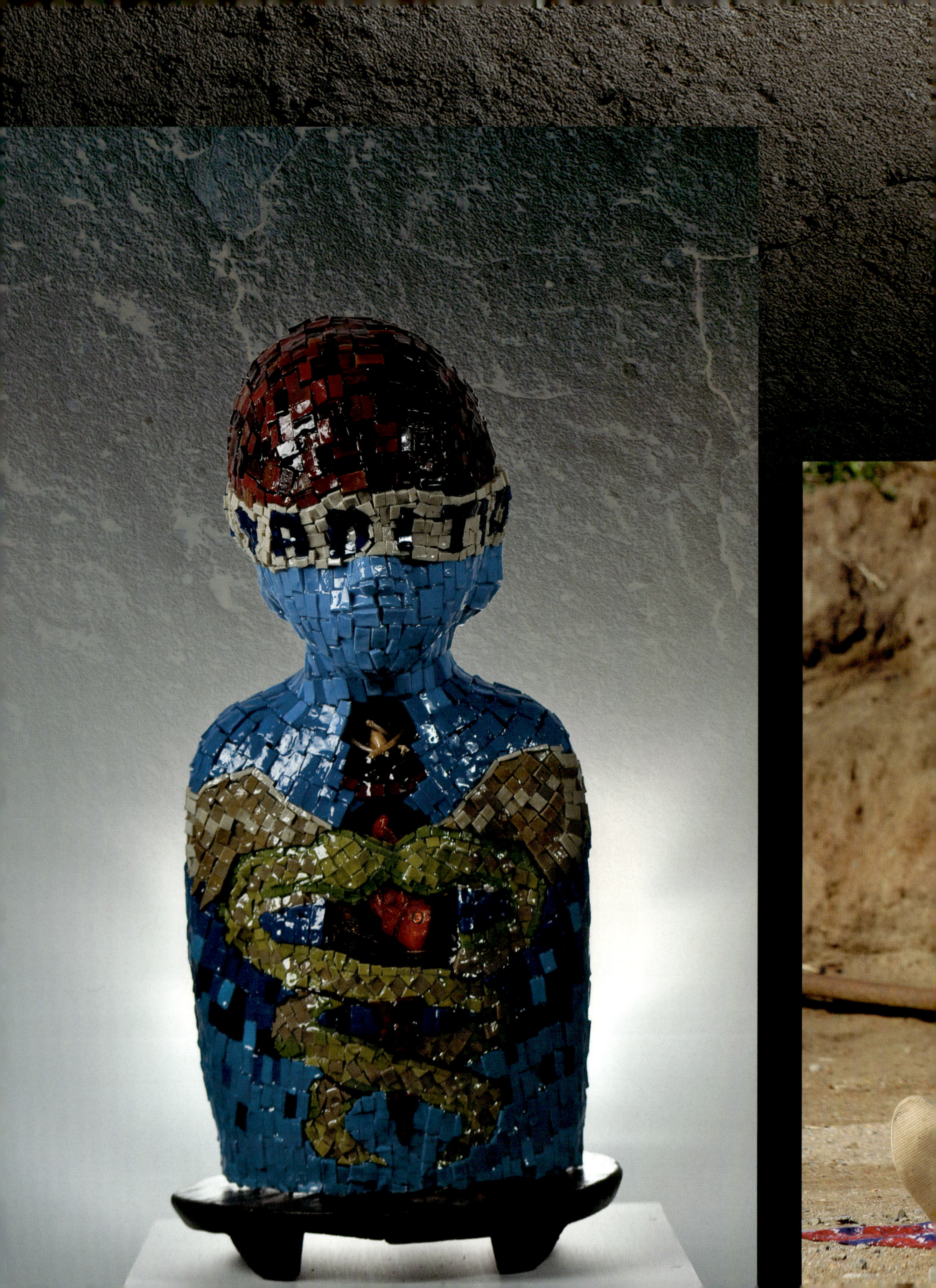

I AM MAMBA AND ORACLE BONES. I AM TRADITION. FROM BEFORE TIME UNDER AZURE AFRICAN SKIES I HAVE REIGNED. NOW MY BALM WILL NOT SOOTHE; MY BONES REST IN DARKNESS. NEW WAYS CONFOUND MY CHILDREN, YET HOPE RESTS ON THE WINGS OF MERCURY. THE ELDER WILL TEACH THE YOUNG THE POWER OF COMMUNITY. THROUGH OUR KINSHIP HEALTH WILL PENETRATE THE BITE OF THIS NEW POISON.

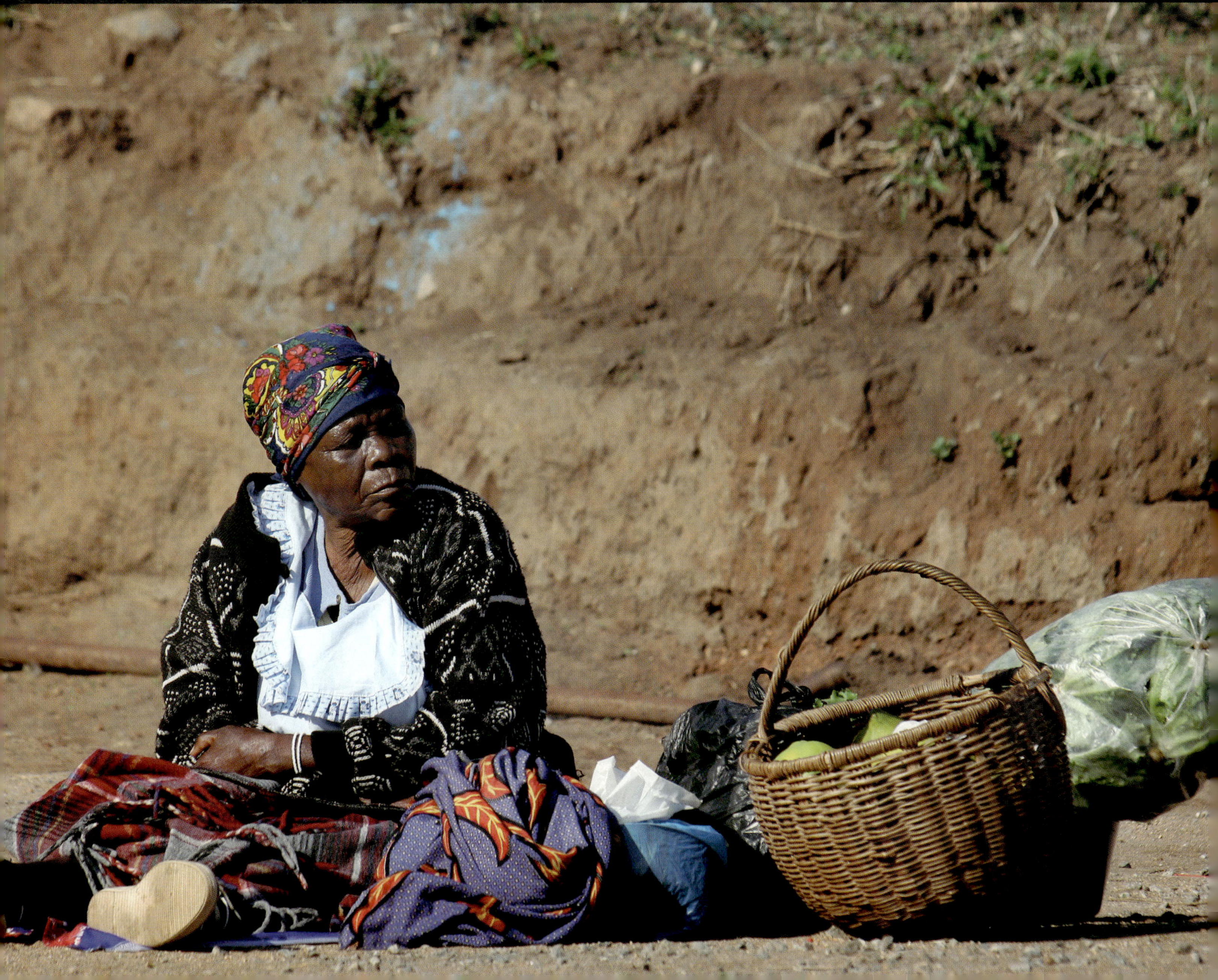

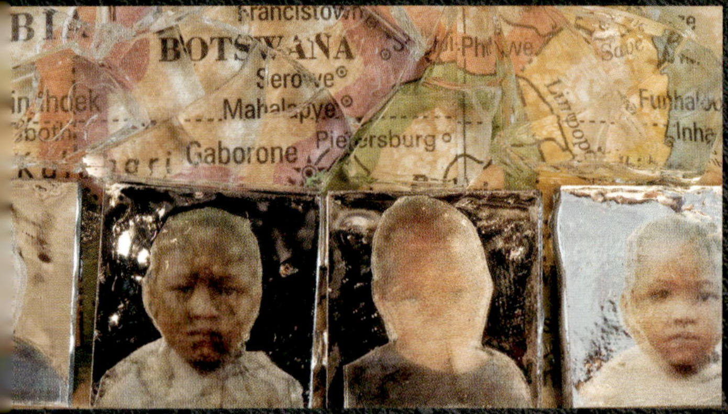
BOTSWANA
Gaborone

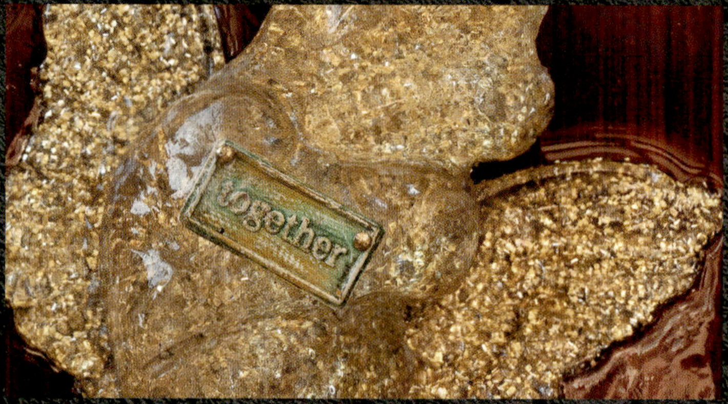
together

"We wander through this life together in a semi-darkness in which none of us can distinguish exactly the features of his neighbour. Only from time to time, through some experience that we have of our companion, or through some remark that he passes, he stands for a moment close to us, as though illuminated by a flash of lightning. Then we see him as he really is."

—ALBERT SCHWEITZER

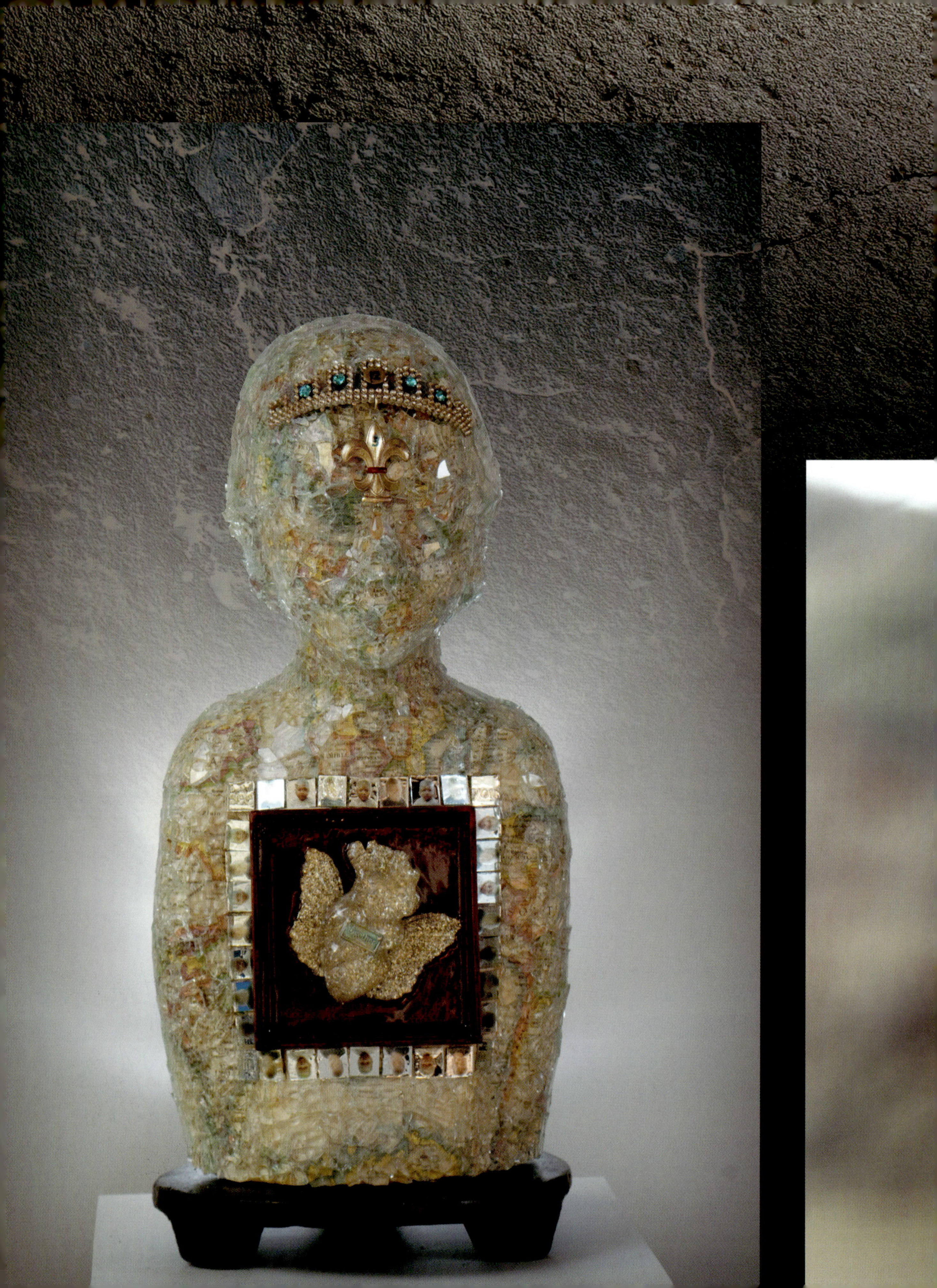

I AM SHATTERED GLASS AND TRANSPARENT HEART. MY EDGES CUT, YOUR EDGES CUT. SEE YOU IN ME? SIDE BY SIDE, AND THE RAZOR'S TONGUE WILL BE SET DOWN. YIELDED, FUSED WE SEIZE THE LIGHT, EMPOWERED; WE WILL UNFURL THE SKIRT OF AURORA. TOGETHER. IF I WOULD RECOGNIZE THE ME IN YOU—THEN YOU WILL BE WELL AND I WILL BE HEALED.

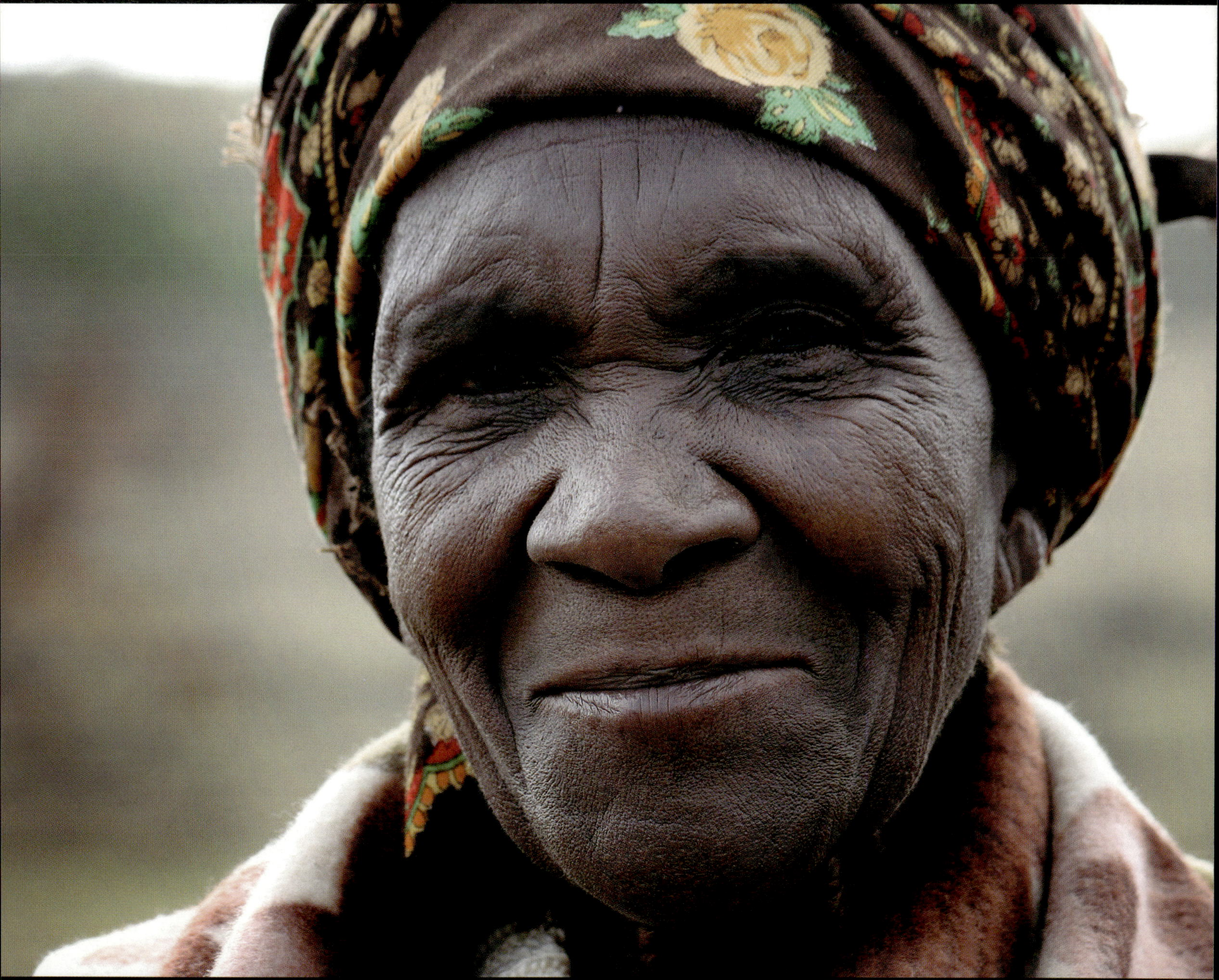

THE GO-GOS

They sit on the bench side by side, arm in arm, four Go-Gos. Go-Go means grandmother in SiSwati. We assume they are related, but we are incorrect.

They are friends; sisters by proxy.

The spokeswoman sits in the middle. Her large toothless grin captures my attention. I immediately like her. She tells me in broken English that she and her "sisters" have lived in the same community for years. They have cared for each other as loved ones have died one after another from AIDS, Tuberculosis (TB), or some other opportunistic disease. No husbands remain. They have either died or left. Only the Go-Gos continue on, each HIV positive, left to care for 19 grandchildren, many of whom are also infected. Indigent and ill, these Go-Gos are the sole matriarch guardians, the only hope for the next generation of their community.

"You care for each other when you are sick. Are you becoming more concerned about caring for each other for fear of catching disease?"

There is a brief silence before they break out in laughter. My question is obviously ludicrous to them.

"We will not stop caring for each other. We take care of each other in every kind of way because we are very, very close neighbors. When something happens to the other one, we will even go to the extent of cooking food for them. And if she is alone, we will sleep with them to make sure she takes her medication. We are so close we know exactly what is happening to the other one. We know what each other needs. We give to each other, and we will lie down with the other until they get up again."

"We have to have food, because without food the ARV (Antiretroviral) drugs will make us very sick."

The Go-Go in the middle points to the woman to her left.

"She went mentally ill for a while because she didn't have food, and she took her meds on an empty stomach. We will share our food even though we don't have enough for ourselves."

"So," she continues, "we will not stop caring for each other. Now it's just a matter of how it must be done. Because before, you didn't wear gloves, you just took care without question. But now, it is a matter of using protective clothing."

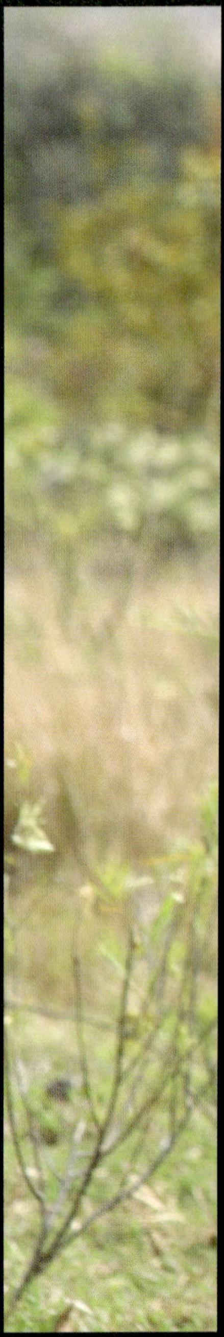

"We will not stop caring for each other."

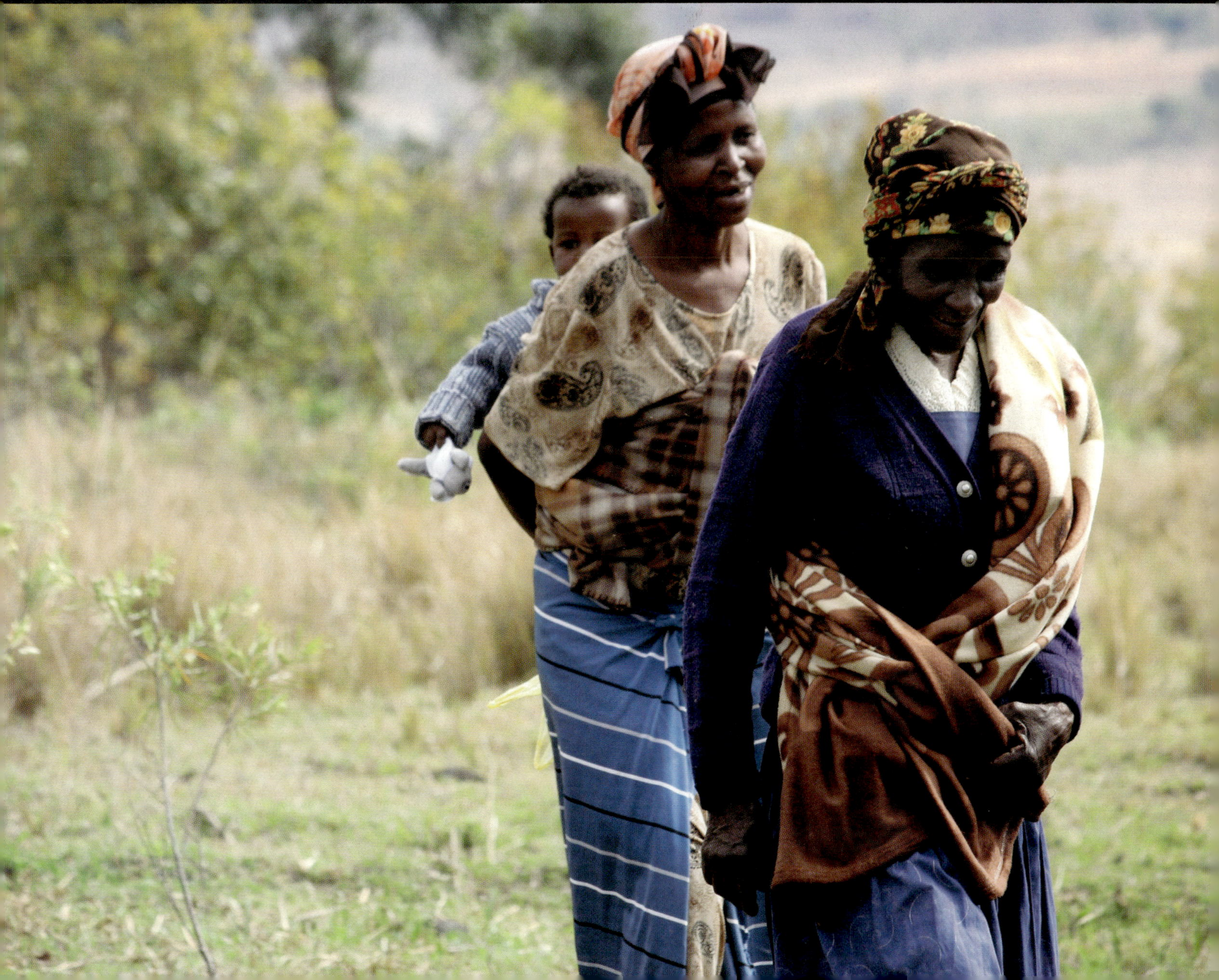

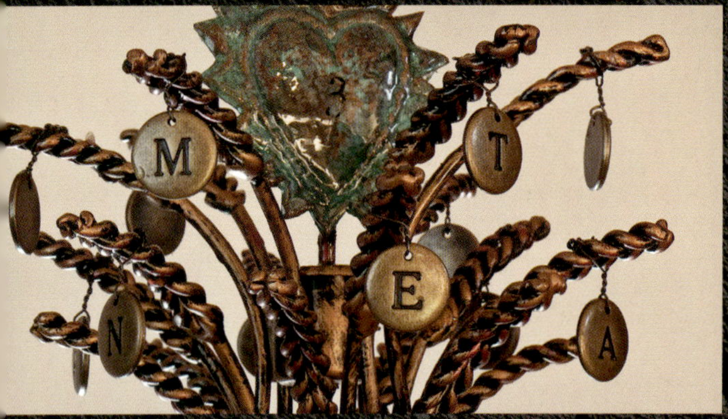
M
T
E
N
A

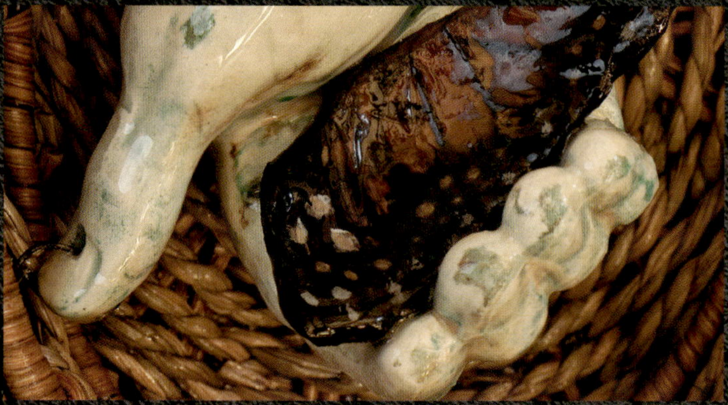

"Peace does not dwell in outward things, but within the soul; we may preserve it in the midst of the bitterest pain, if our will remains firm and submissive. Peace in this life springs from acquiescence to, not in an exemption from, suffering."

—FRANCOIS DE FENELON

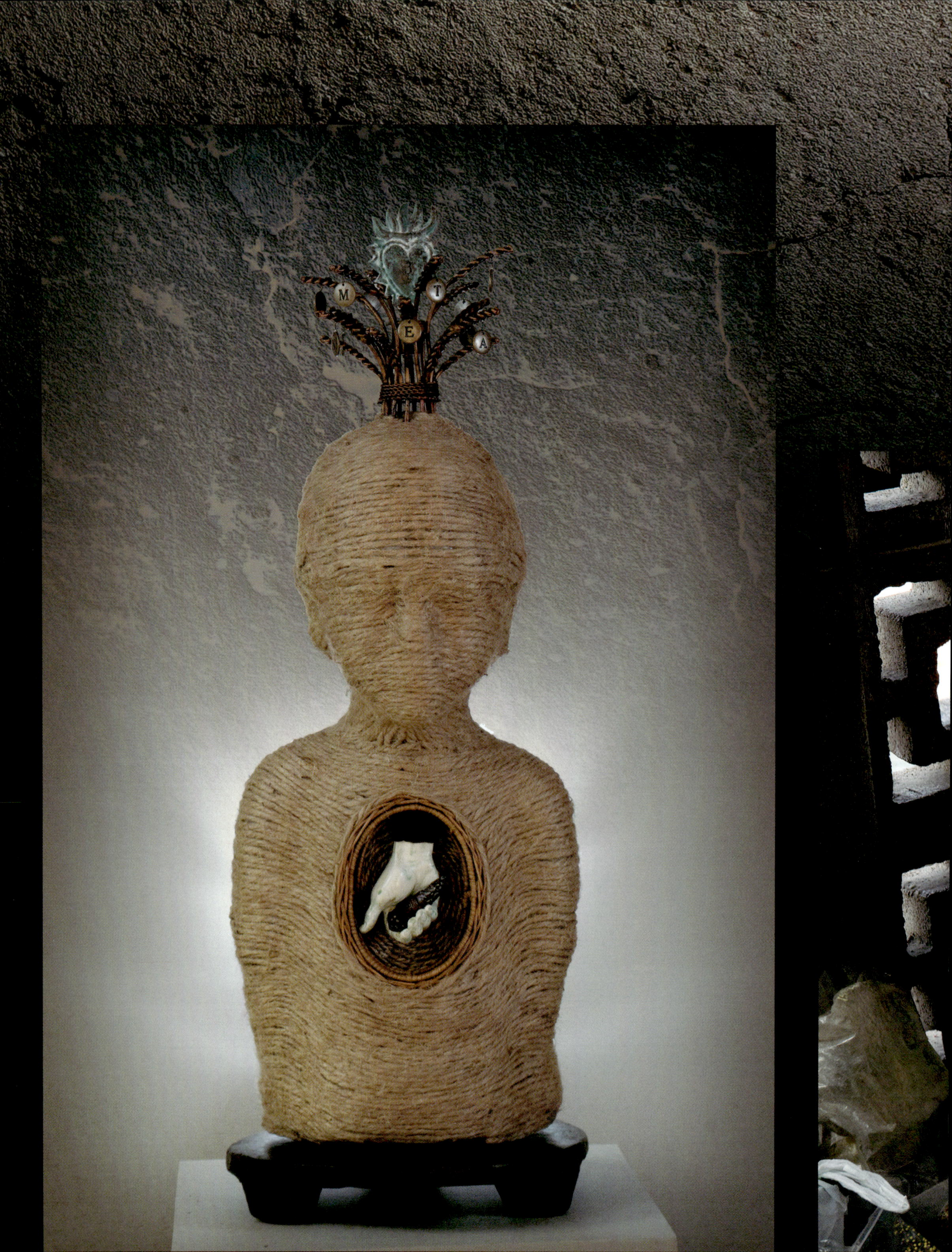

I AM A JUTE COCOON AND A NEW WING. SURVIVAL DANCES BENEATH MY EMACIATED CAST WHERE ANTICIPATION FEEDS THE LARVAE OF TOMORROW. SUFFERING CANNOT COMPETE WITH THE CALM BENEATH THE TIES. METAMORPHOSIS BEGINS AT THE CORE. MY SOUL SWELLS AND SOON WILL NO LONGER SUBMIT TO THE CONSTRAINTS OF THIS PRESENT LIFE. I WILL PUT ON MY NEW WINGS AND GATHER FLIGHT.

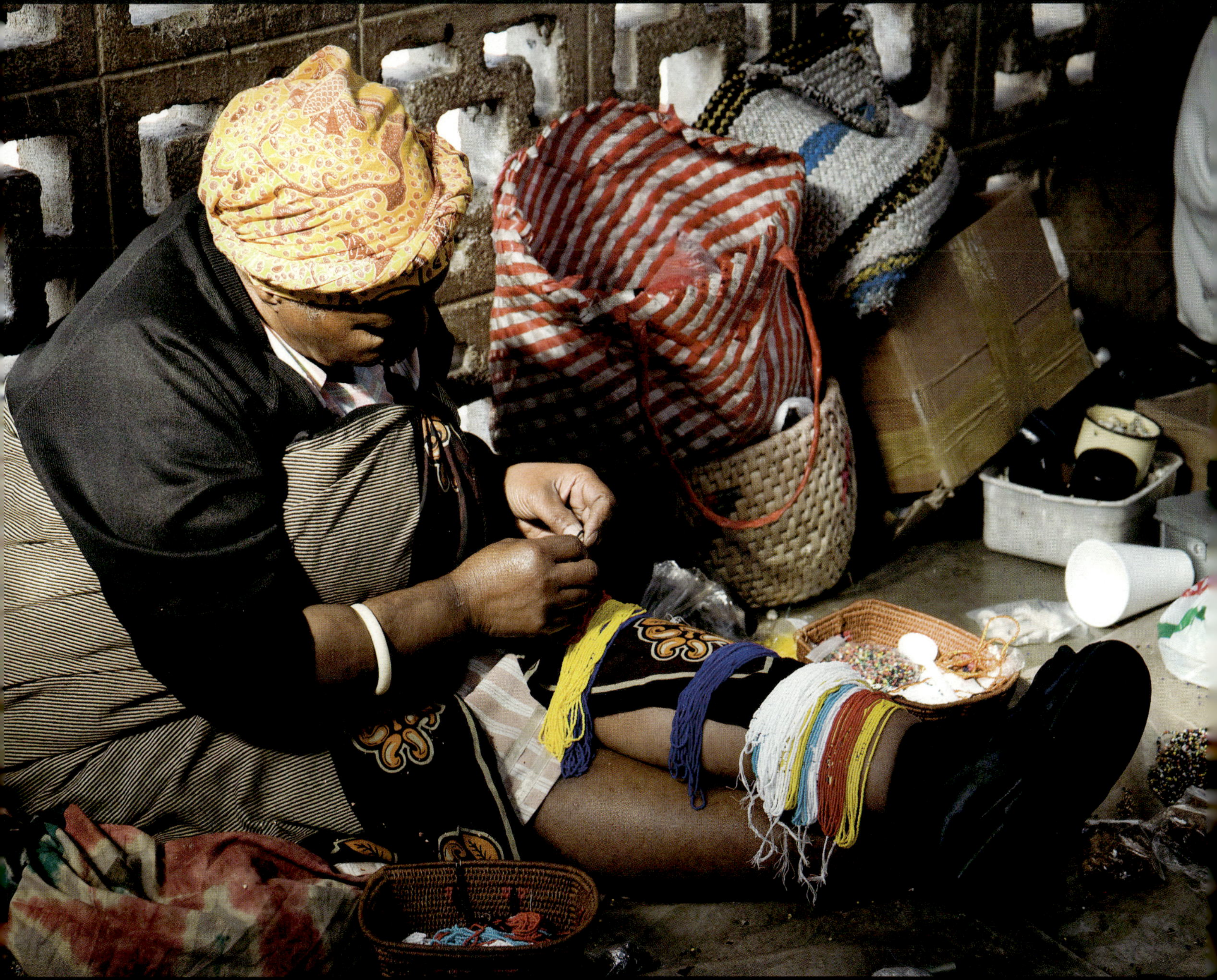

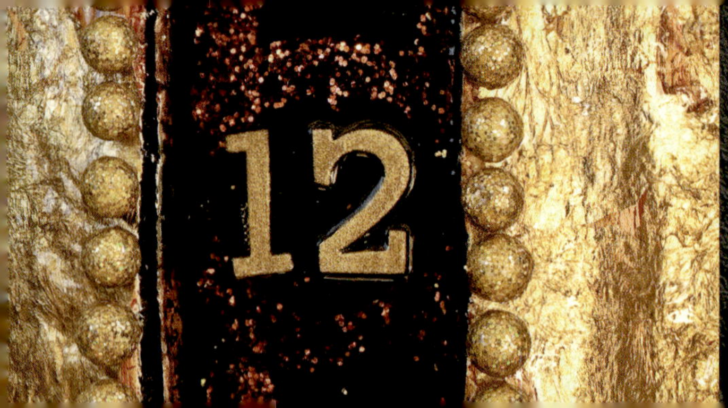
12
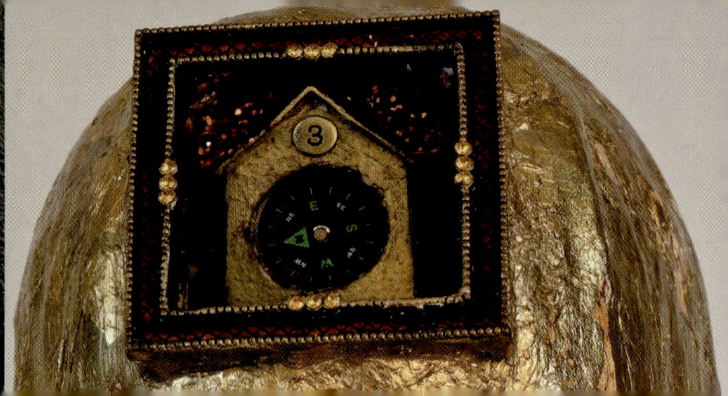
3
E
S
W

"Here bring your wounded hearts, here tell your anguish;
Earth has no sorrow that Heaven cannot heal."

—THOMAS MORE

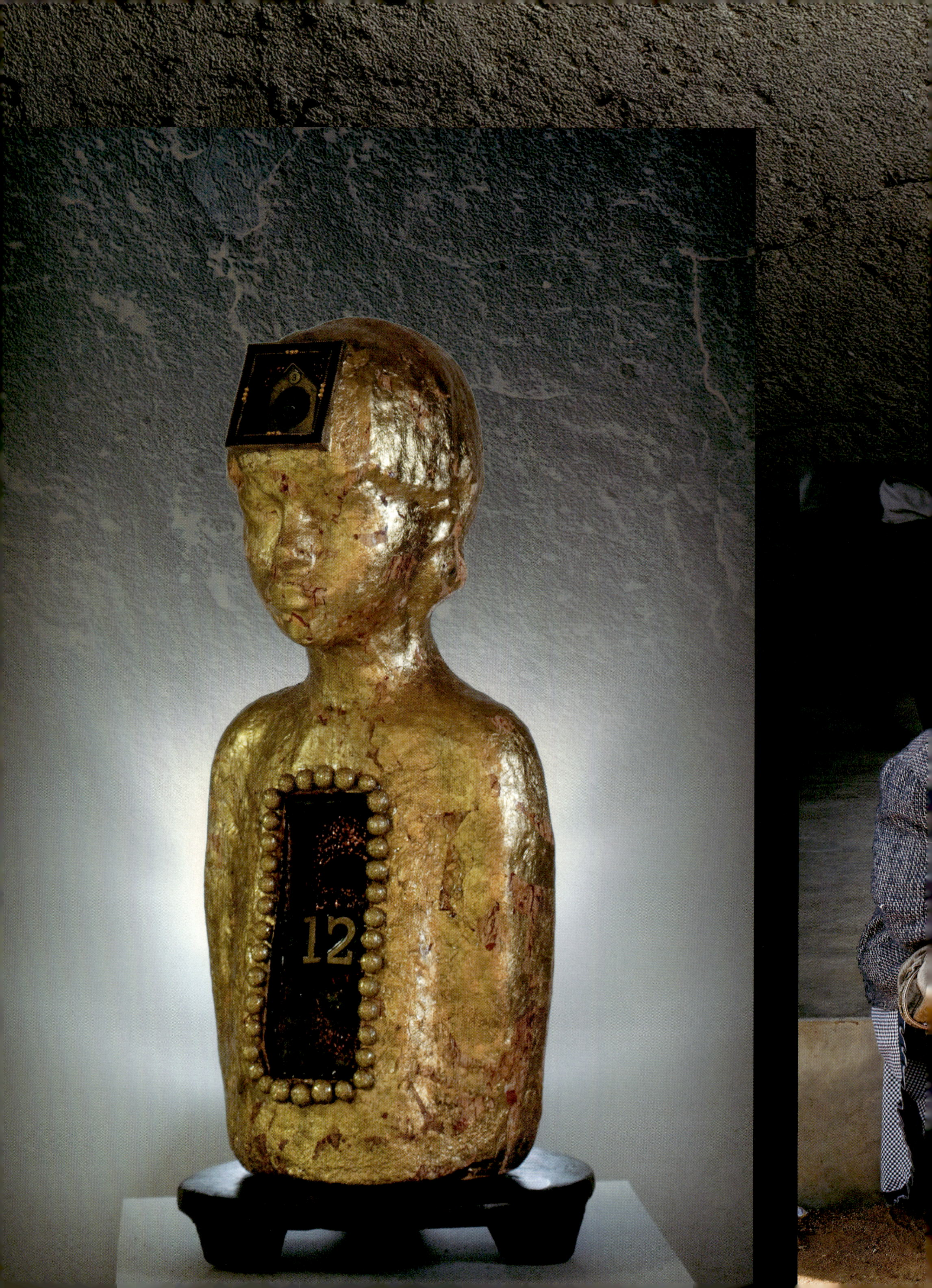
12

I AM THE GOLDEN ORATOR, THE KEEPER OF LIFE'S STORY. MY MEMORY SKIN IS MARKED. VESTIGES STING THE SURFACE, PURGED BY A GOLDEN ACHE. A GATHERING SOJOURNER, I BUT REFLECT THE STORIES IN US ALL. OH, MERCY COMPENSATE MY HEELLESS SLIPPERS. FAITH, CONSUME THE DROSS. MY COMPASS IS STAYED. AT THE END OF THIS DAY, I AM GOING HOME.

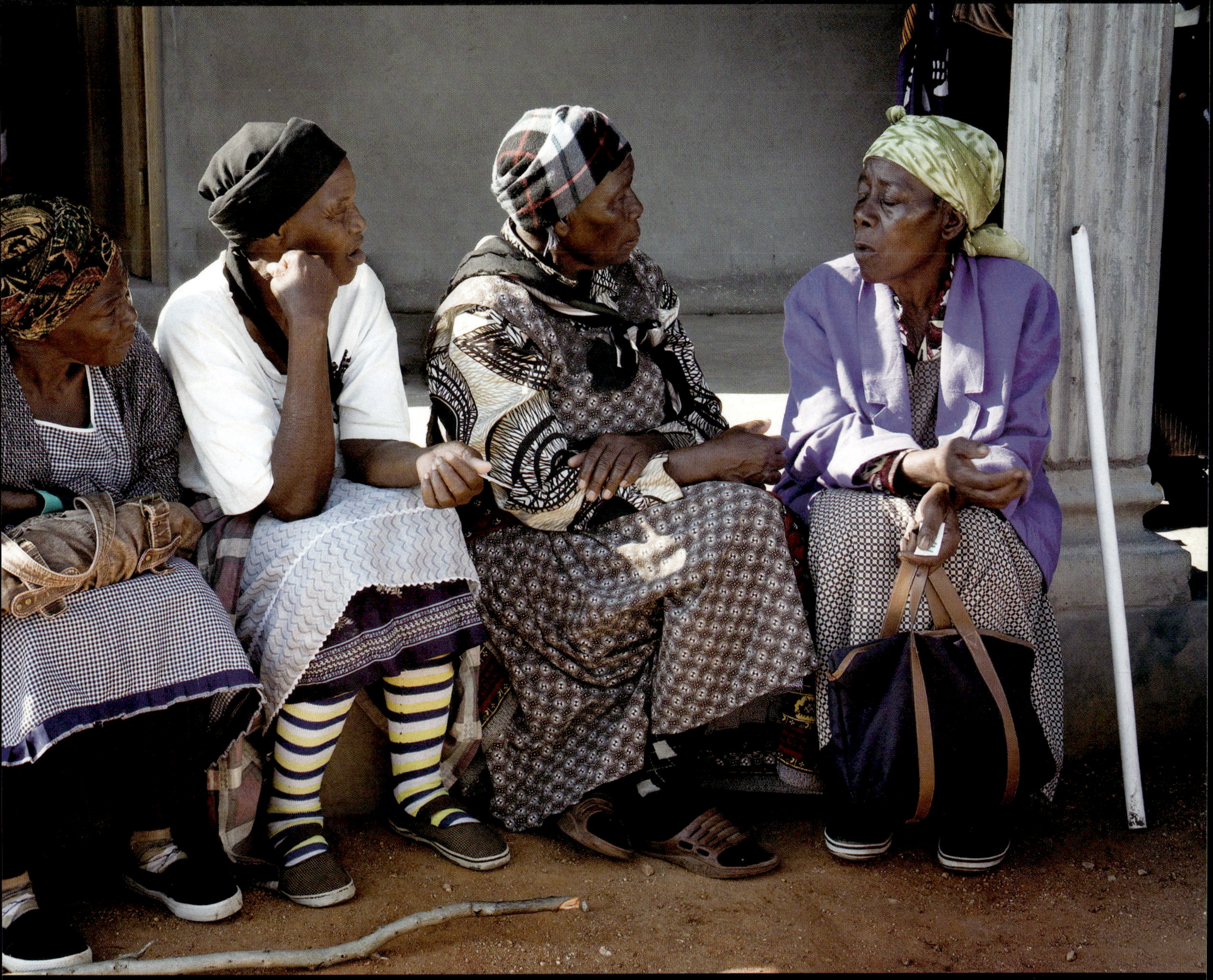

WOMEN IN BLACK

She dances, with the infant strapped to her back; her body sways to the sound of children's voices. Dressed entirely in black, she first caught my eye as she tended to the large cast iron pot at GiGi's place. As the children are served, they sing and she dances. I inquire as to who she is. "She is the woman in black," I am told. "She is cooking today so that her children can eat and she is in mourning for her husband. It is tradition. Her husband died of AIDS."

"For the first one to two months after her husband's death, a woman lives in a special hut by herself. She has no furniture, only a mat and blankets. She sleeps or sits on the ground. She is not allowed to do any cooking, shopping, or anything outside of the homestead. Any time a man enters the house where she is staying, she must cover her face. After this period of time is over, the widow is fitted for her "widow's garb." Traditionally, women are supposed to wear this for two years."

I think about this.

If a black shroud is a symbol for mourning the women of Swaziland would be completely justified in covering themselves in darkness every day. There are so many difficulties to face in this impoverished nation. Disease, lack of food and medicine, extreme environments, and little to no water would be bad enough, but if you are a woman, the odds are even greater. They are stacked against you.

According to a recent commissioned UNICEF and CDC study, "One in three girls in Swaziland has experienced sexual violence by age 18. In addition, researchers found that 22% of Swazi women between ages 15 and 24 are HIV-positive, noting that sexual violence could

The Swazi culture demands that women (and girls) bear this abuse in silence. So they do. Recent findings show that 67% of women are suffering from depression.

Tradition also states that the land and the inheritance will go to the son, not the daughter. So, women in Swaziland are economically pressured to get married so that they will not end up homeless. Women are often forced to prove they can bear children before a man will marry them.

Polygamy is traditional in Swaziland. Suppose a man has three wives and ten children, and he and two wives end up dying of AIDS. This leaves the remaining wife who is likely HIV positive herself to take care of all the children. Eventually, without proper care and nutrition, she will die and leave the children as orphans. Unfortunately, this scenario is not uncommon. The results are catastrophic on a national level where over 150,000 orphaned children have been left behind. This next generation is at risk, and the women—the mothers—know this. They carry this emotional burden every day.

Given all this, I would assume black cloth and ashes would be appropriate attire. This is not the opinion of the Swazi women, however. Black is reserved for mourning. The women of Swaziland prefer to wear the brightest most brilliant colors. Like bouquets of flowers they color their communities—their daily lives with hope—and they choose to dance even among dire circumstances.

"This next generation is at risk, and the women—the mothers—know this. They carry this emotional burden every day."

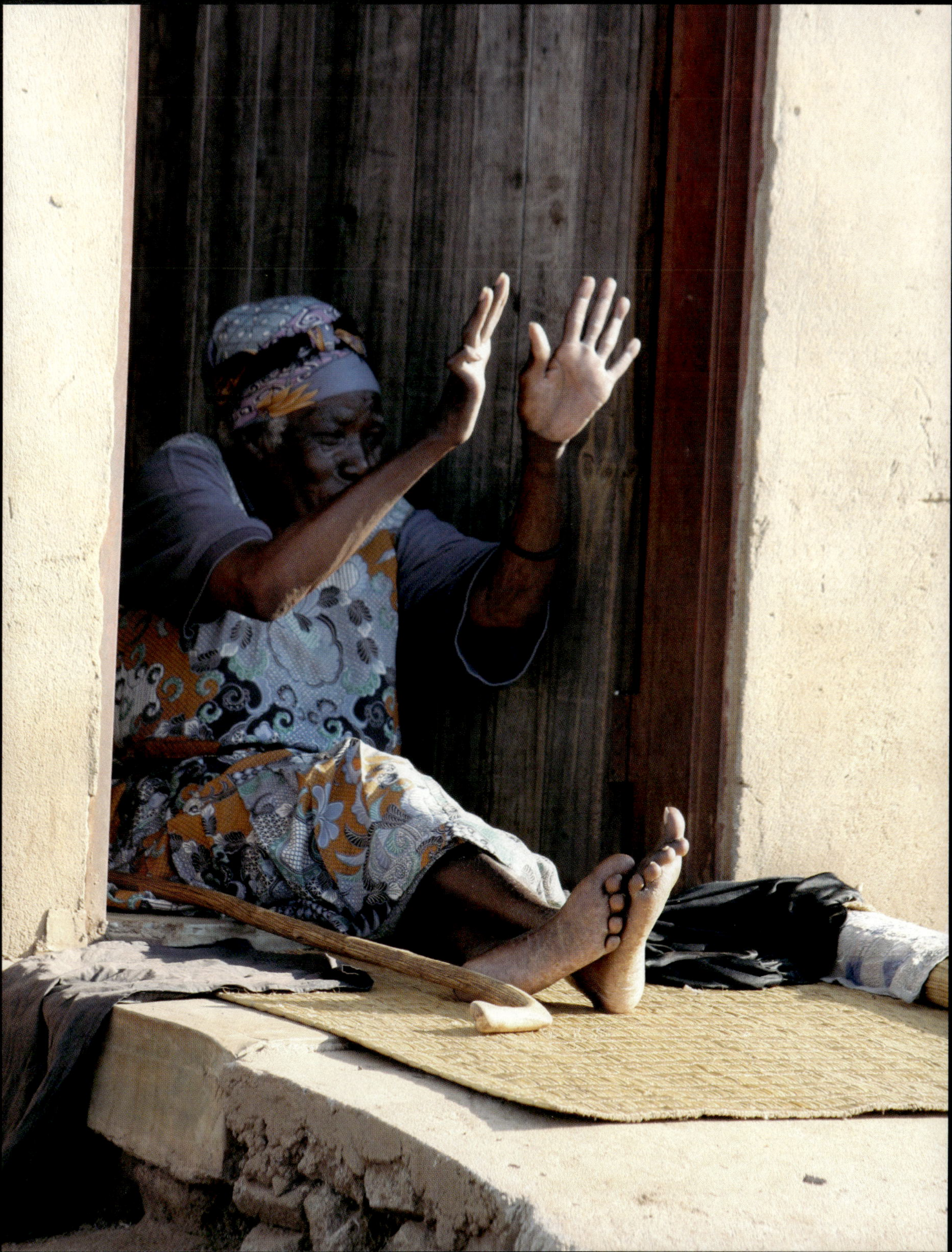

GIGI'S KIDS EXHIBIT

Artists Respond

A secondary exhibit was developed to take part during the inaugural showing of *Lizinga Lemandla Ami: The Measure of My Strength*. While in Swaziland, Bridget and Eric captured hundreds of images of the most vulnerable—the children served at Gigi's Place. Each time we visited Gigi's Place, we left with the haunting images of the children burned on our hearts. We discussed the potential of using the pictures of the children as the inspiration for the creation of art. Ultimately, we chose to create an invitational exhibit involving a variety of genres represented by 24 artists. This exhibit was developed specifically to raise funds in support of the mission of Gigi's Place, and provide nutrition and education for the hundreds of orphans and street children living in the slums of Manzini, Swaziland.

Out of hundreds of photos taken of children at Gigi's Place, Bridget and Eric selected 25 to 30 images. Each invited artist was asked to choose one of the images of a child from this gallery of photos. Each artist received an image of the child they selected. We then asked each artist to use the photo in their studio as inspiration while working on their piece of art. Each artist created a single piece of art in honor of the child they chose. At the exhibit, the images of the children were elevated to the wall, mounted on canvas. Each work of art was displayed next to its inspiration—the haunting image of one of Gigi's kids.

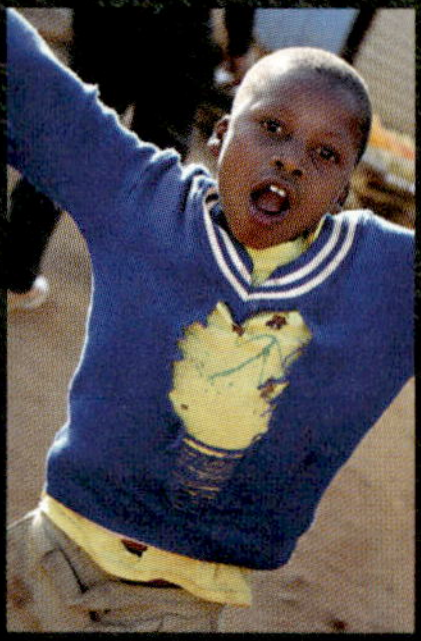

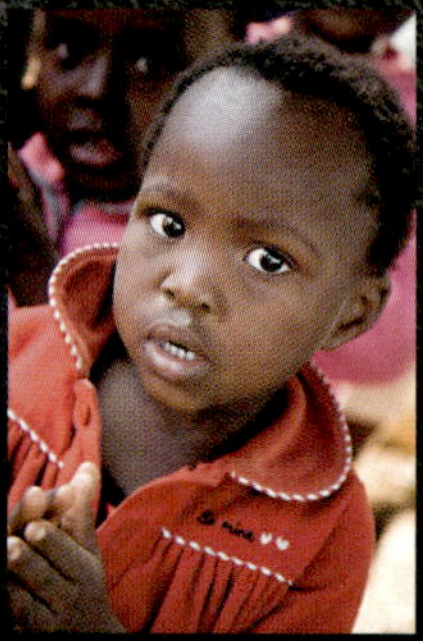

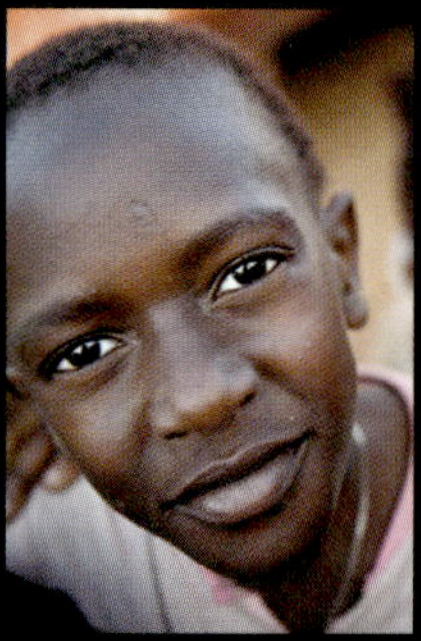

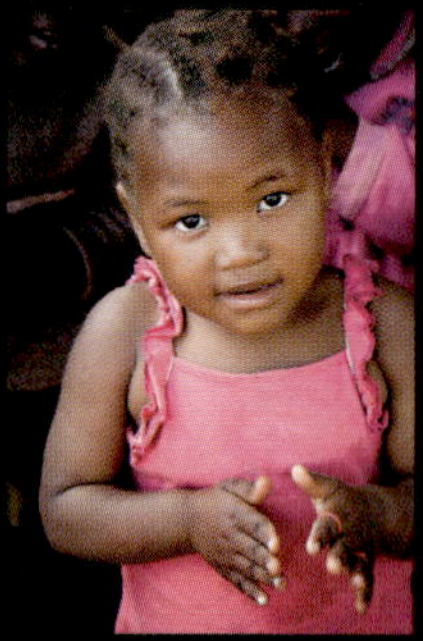

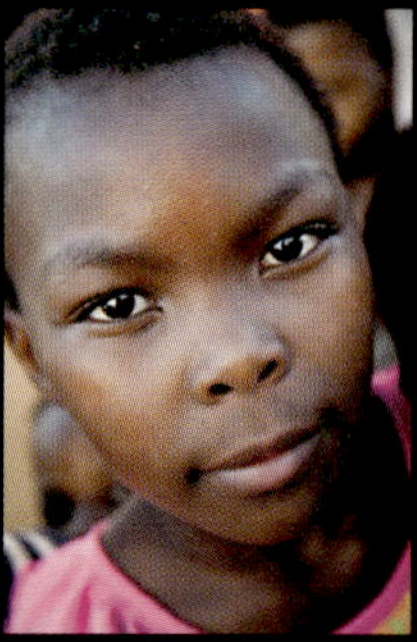

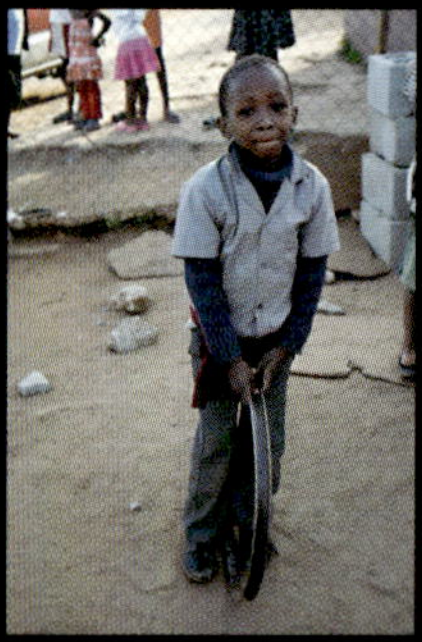

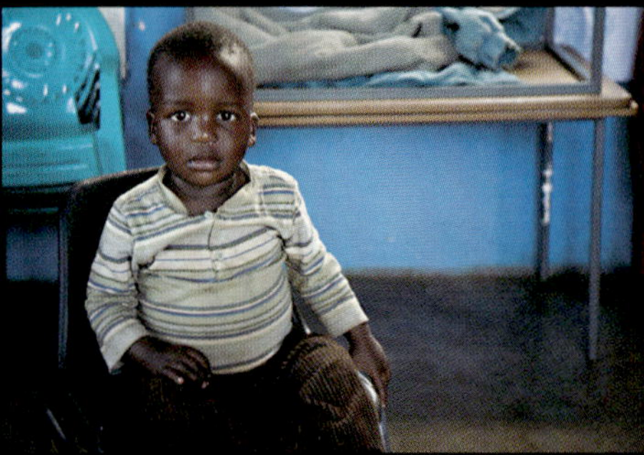

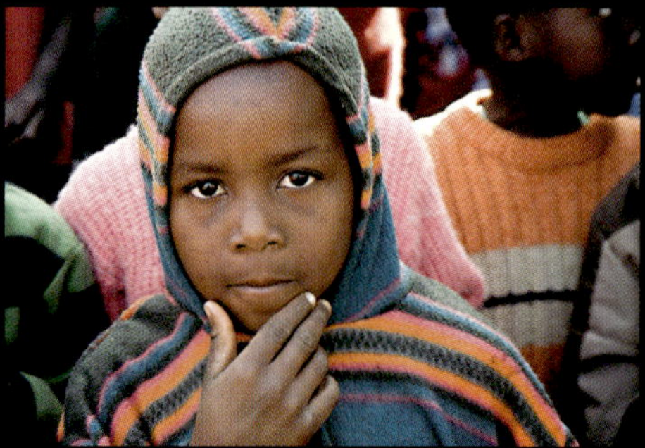

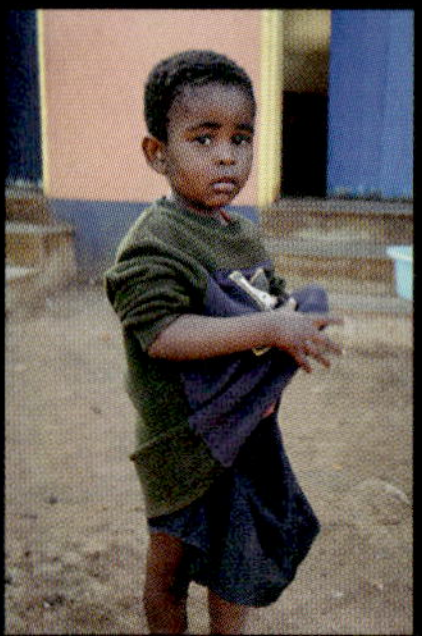

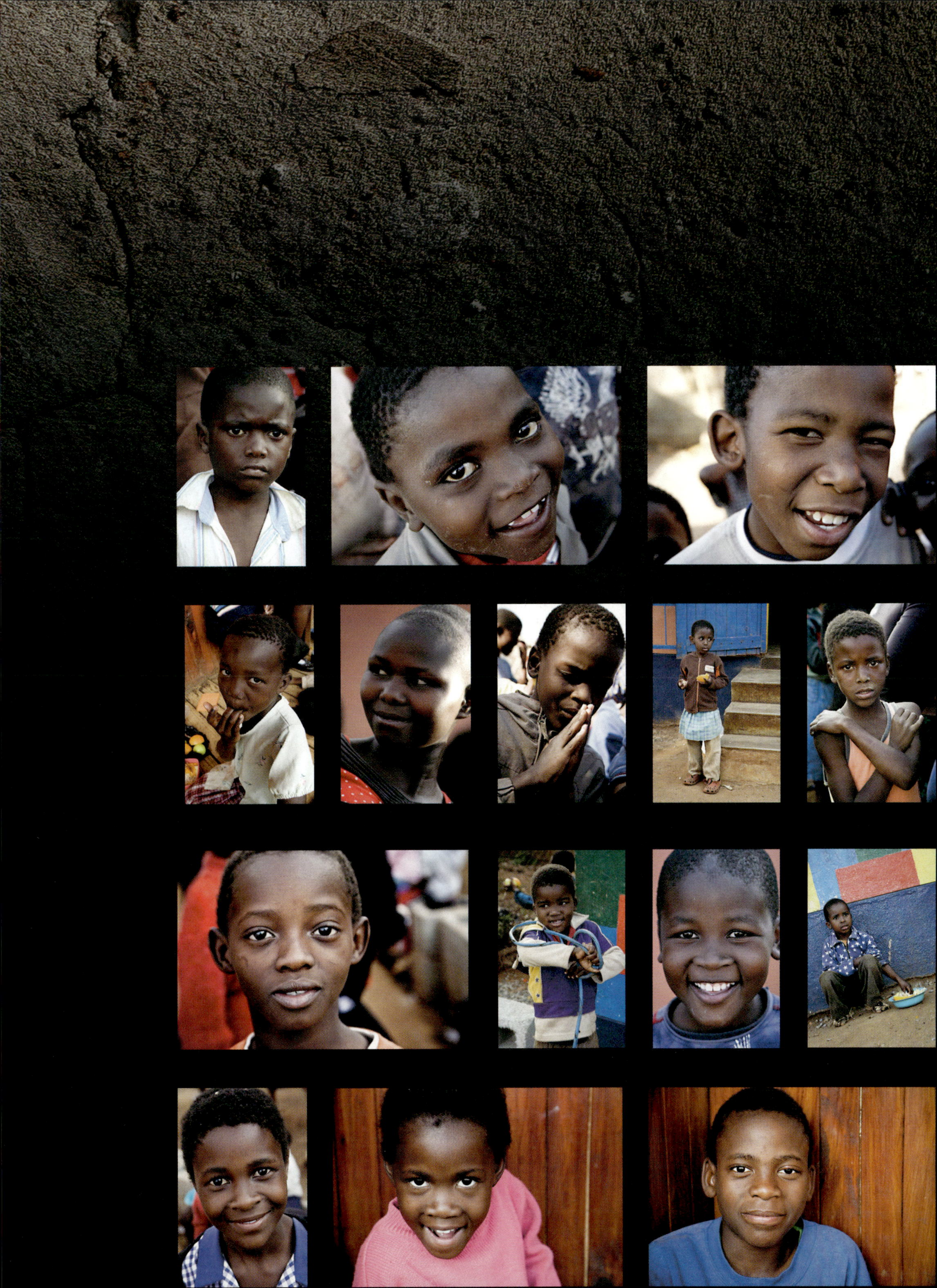

GIGI'S KIDS EXHIBIT PHOTOGRAPHER STATEMENT

Eric and Bridget Pipkin

Our travels to Swaziland, Africa, brought us a renewed understanding of joy, strength, and humility in a seemingly devastated land.

In a small Swaziland community nestled in the heart of Manzini lies a source of refuge for hundreds of orphaned and homeless children. GiGi's Place is filled with love, laughter, and generosity. Children wait every day outside a gated fence lined with barbed wire anticipating nourishment for their bodies, minds, and hearts. Three o'clock arrives and only a limited number of these children are allowed through the gates. Modeling love, local volunteers are there to lead these children through songs of praise and words of wisdom in remembering what ultimately to be grateful for. A bowl of beans and porridge line the tummies of these children who have endured so much. Looking around, we are astonished to see children sacrificially passing their food through the fence to other children who are facing the same brutal circumstances. Selfless, these children teach us the true meaning of compassion.

These amazing children from GiGi's Place reveal a true sense of joy that surpasses their painful conditions. They teach us about the abundance of life, gratitude, and generosity within community. But just as we need them to remind us about the true meaning of life, they desperately need our support in healthcare, medicine, water, and nutrition. Devastated but not completely broken, the future of Swaziland lies in the hopes and dreams displayed in the children of GiGi's Place and in the measure of their strength.

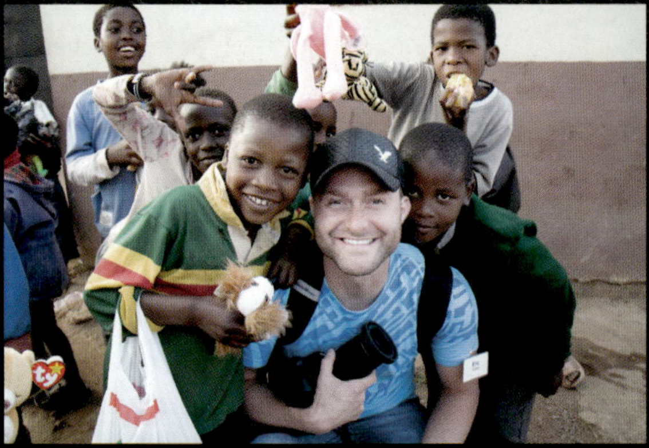

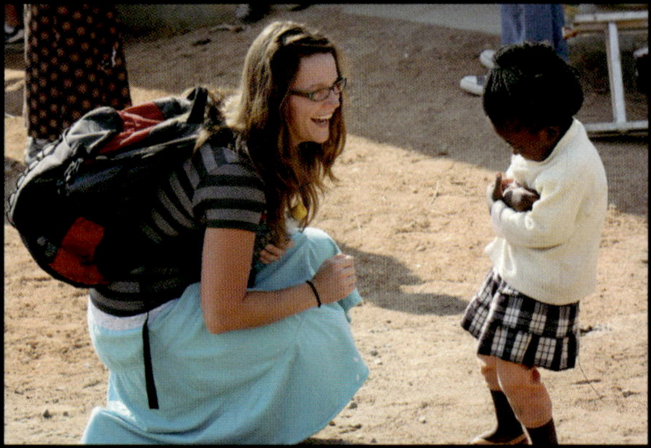

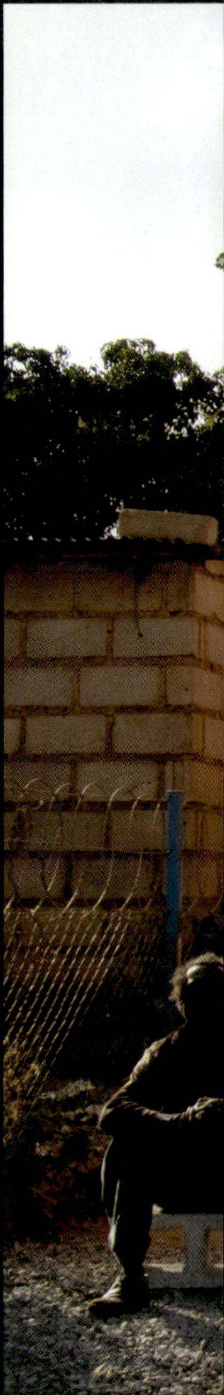

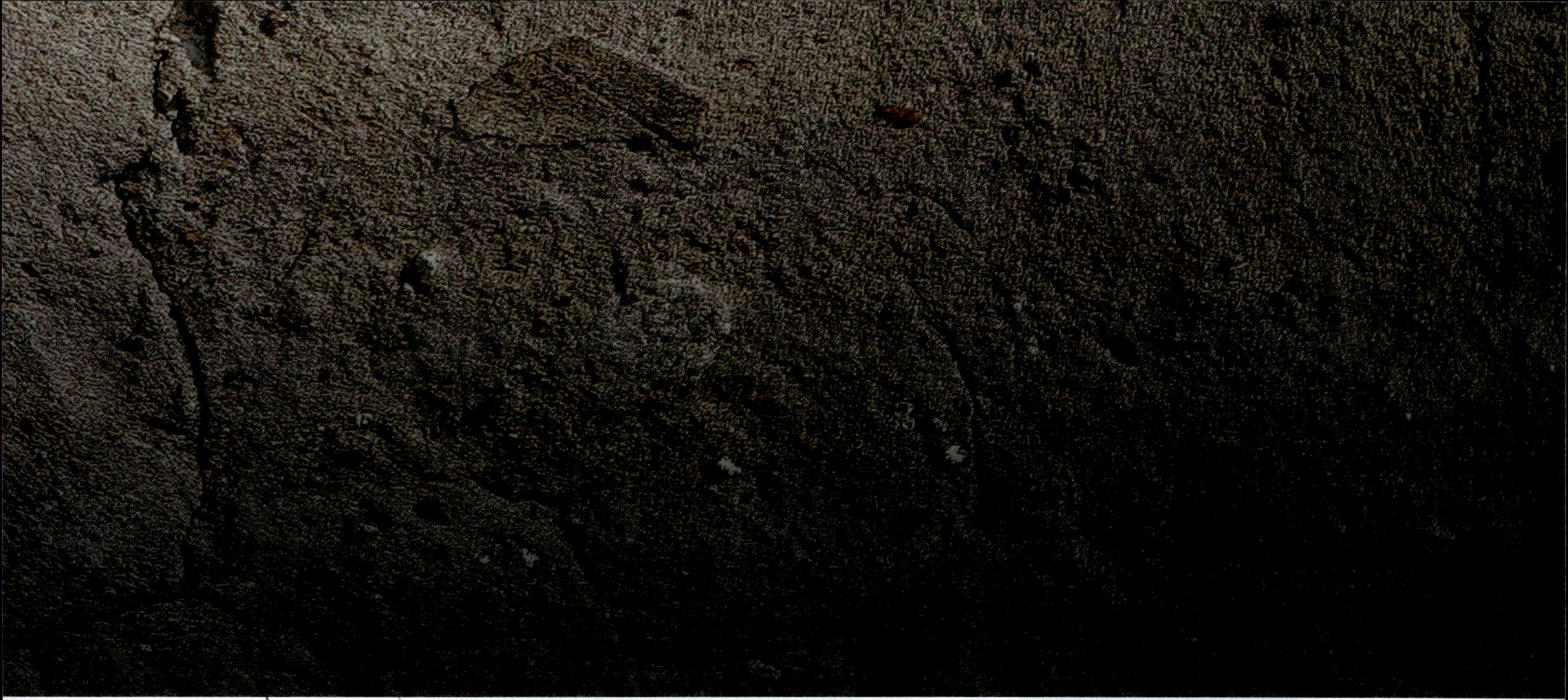

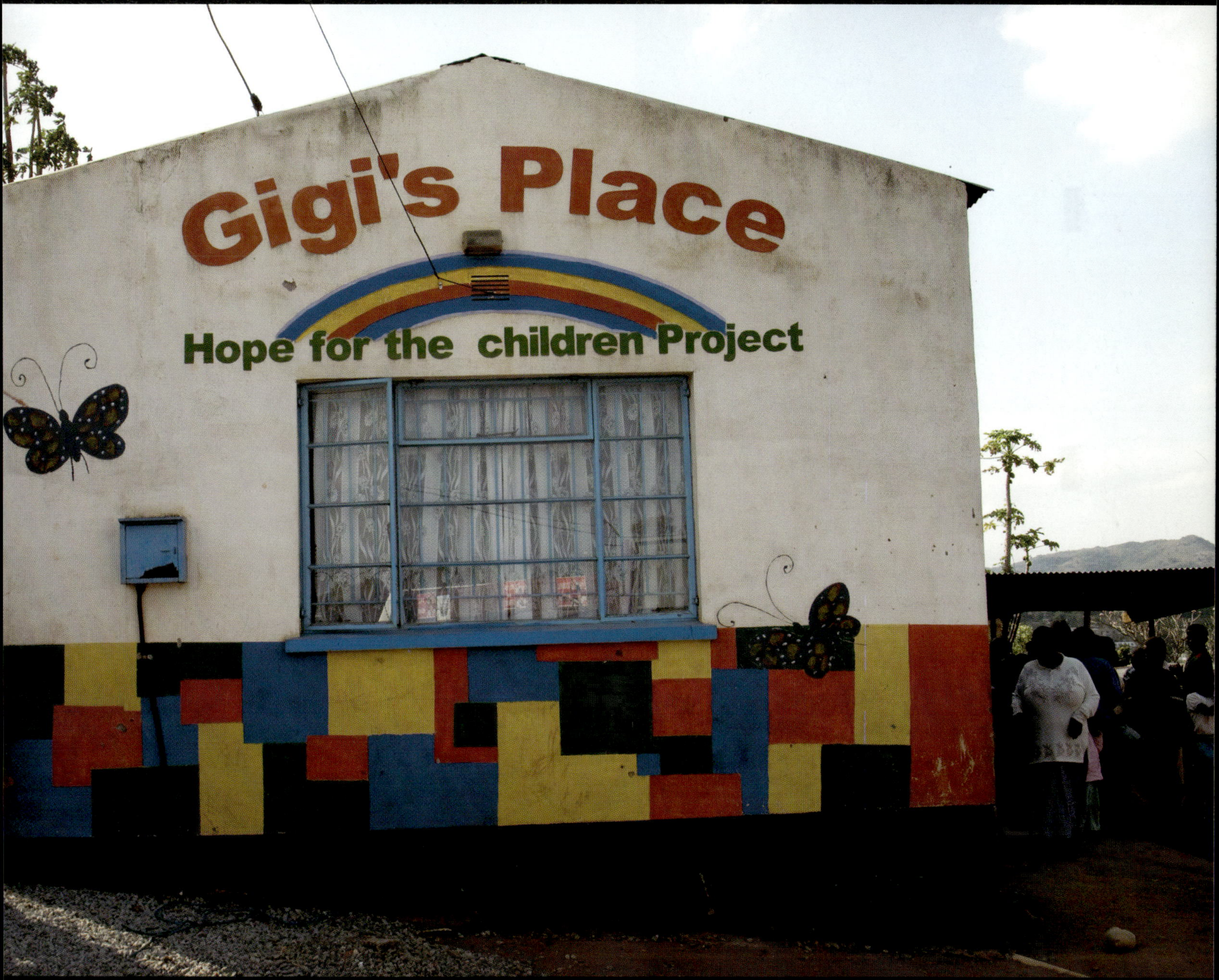
Gigi's Place
Hope for the children Project

GIGI'S KIDS
Artists' Statements

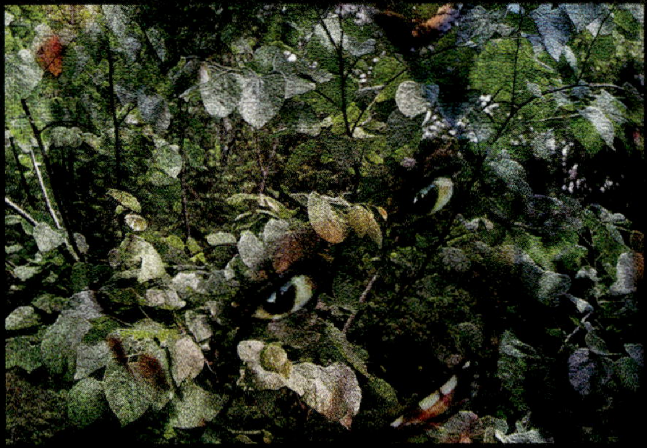

M. Teresa Valero
Eyes Tell All
Color Photography

"My child (#17) was immediately appealing to me because of his beautiful smile and engaging expression. How can I bring this child home? How can I make his image relevant to me? After much consideration, I settled on the idea of a background pattern. Nothing more fitting than the Eastern Redbud which is the state tree of Oklahoma. I was looking to merge two images and to create a new one. One that will give the feeling of rebirth and hope. If you look carefully in the child's eyes you can see a viewer's (photographer's) reflection that is you, me, us, we the people who care for the children and women of Swaziland and who are changing their future."

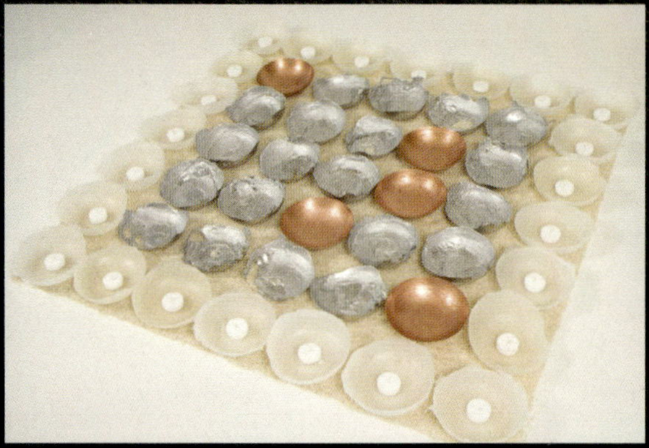

Shawn Meyers
The Measure of a Life
Mixed Media Sculpture Installation

"My youngest son most probably would not live to be the age of my oldest son if they had been born in Swaziland. These small "begging bowls" represent the one boy in five or the five out of 25 who will survive into adulthood. Five hammered copper bowls, their color representing life, glint in the midst of 20 lead bowls, their dull toxicity representing death. All are nestled on a bed of rice, often the only food these children receive in a day. Surrounding this visceral arrangement are 25 fragile beeswax bowls, each containing a burning candle. These bowls, soon to be consumed, represent the lives already lost to this epidemic."

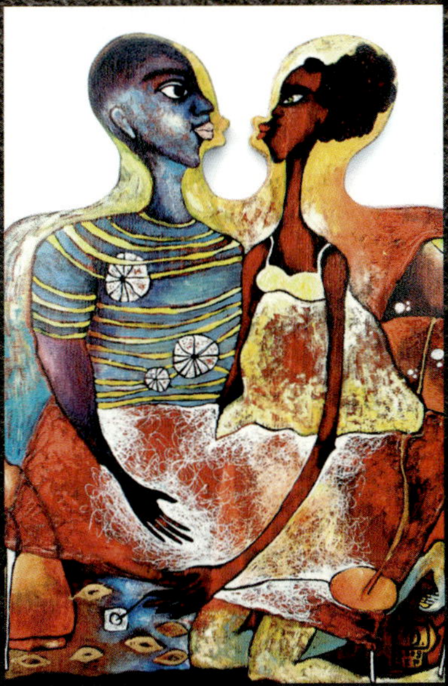

Tunde Darvey
Forgiveness
Mixed Media

"In this painting, I give visual expression to the vital importance of friendship, love, and intimacy in every day life. Cherishing these notions helps us create dialogues across cultures, dialogues that are the building blocks of a global world that simultaneously connects and isolates people with different backgrounds."

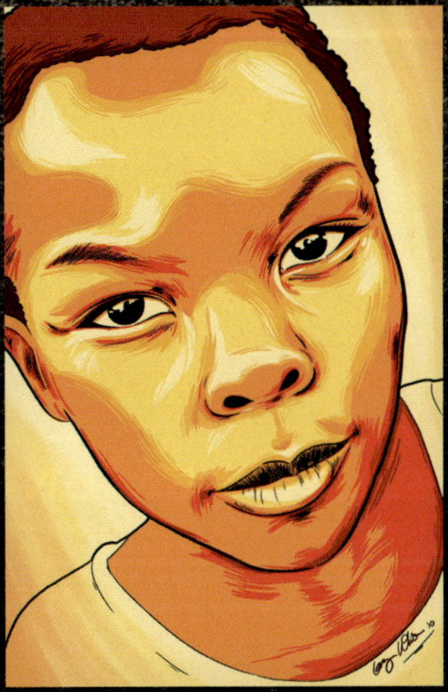

Greg White
Untitled
Digital

"When I saw the picture of this little girl, I was struck by her piercing eyes. In constructing this piece, I wanted to emphasize that by choosing a style and color palette that would get the viewer's attention and draw them in."

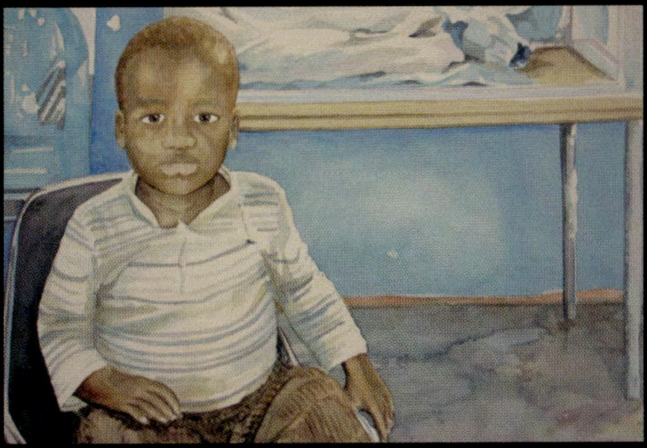

Steven Coy
Created for Purpose
Watercolor

"My heart went out to the boy I saw in the photograph. I felt sympathy for his suffering, but also saw his gentle, quiet spirit. The colors of blue exemplify both the melancholy in his eyes and the brightness of hope for his future."

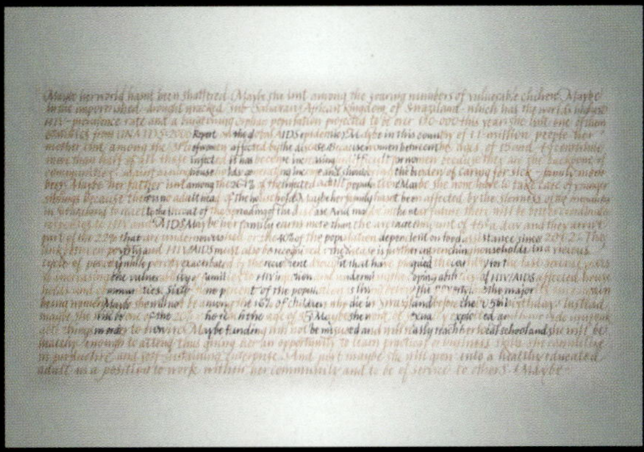

Karyn L. Gilman
Just Maybe
Calligraphy

"I looked at this picture and wondered about what this young girl had to look forward to in her future. She had food in front of her, it gave me hope that just maybe she could escape some of the worst statistics."

ACKNOWLEDGEMENTS

This project has been funded in part by:

Special thanks to the following organizations and individuals who have contributed either funds, goods or services, making *Lizinga Lemandla Ami: The Measure of My Strength* possible.

KIRKPATRICK FOUNDATION, INC.

INDIVIDUAL ARTISTS OF OKLAHOMA

OKLAHOMA VISUAL ARTS COALITION

BETHANY FIRST CHURCH OF THE NAZARENE

SOUTHERN NAZARENE UNIVERSITY

Organizations

www.AnnShermanPhoto.com
www.ExhibitConcepts.com
Foto Arts Photography
Gigi's Place
Mercer Associates, Inc.
McKinley Hardwoods, LLC
The Swaziland HIV/AIDS Task Force
The Swaziland Partnership
Tate Publishing & Enterprises, LLC
True Color Photo

Individuals

Caryn Adams
Pat Burton
Jon and Karla Cargill
Margaret Eaton
Marcia Feisal
Fayth Fitzgerald
Elizabeth Forman
Gwen Ladd Hackler
Brent and Michaele LaVigne
Kelley Lunsford
Mary Magagula
Rita McClain
Gary Mercer
Danica Mercer
Bob W. Miller
Rev. Harlan and Barbi Moore
Ryan "Staples" Scott
Evelyn Shongwe
The Women of Swaziland
Alan W. Wyett
Kevin Wyett

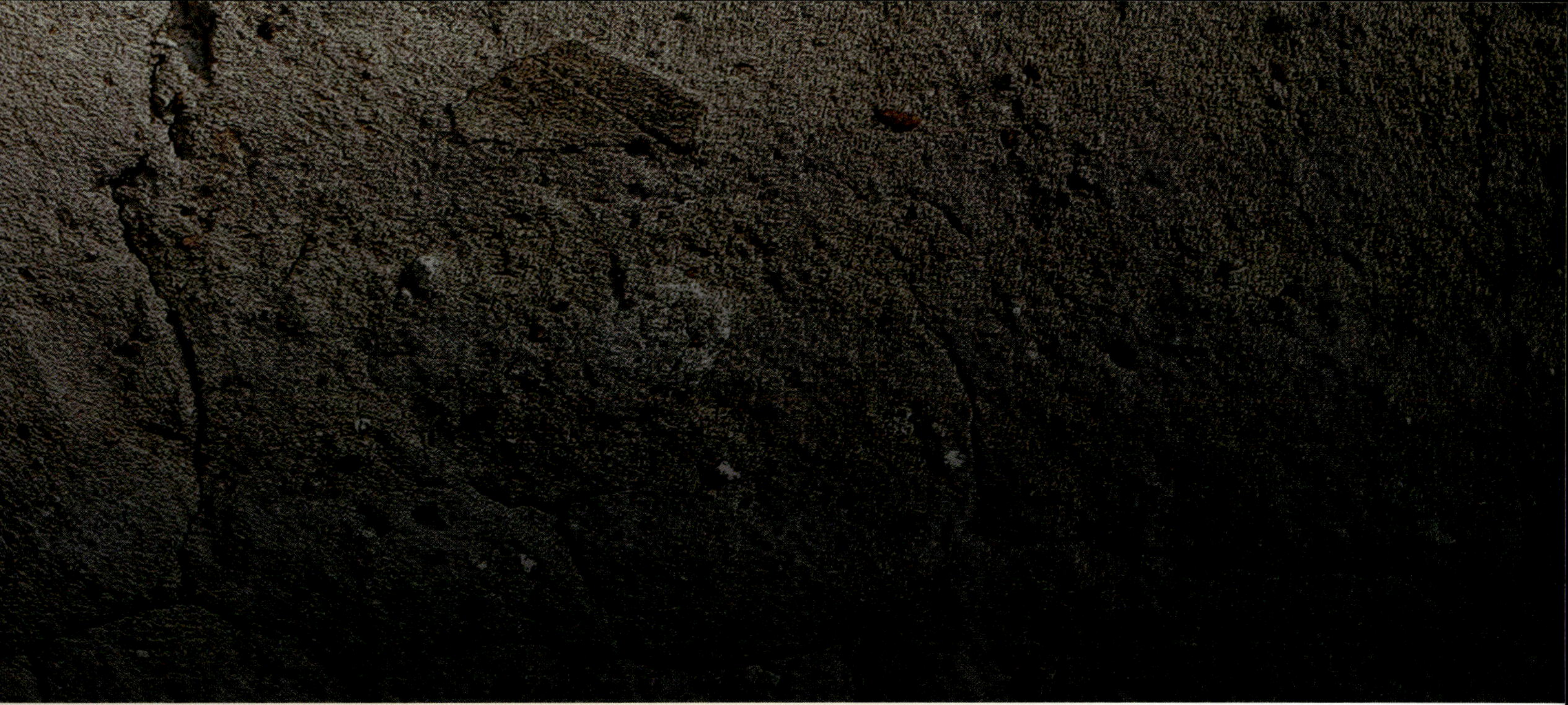

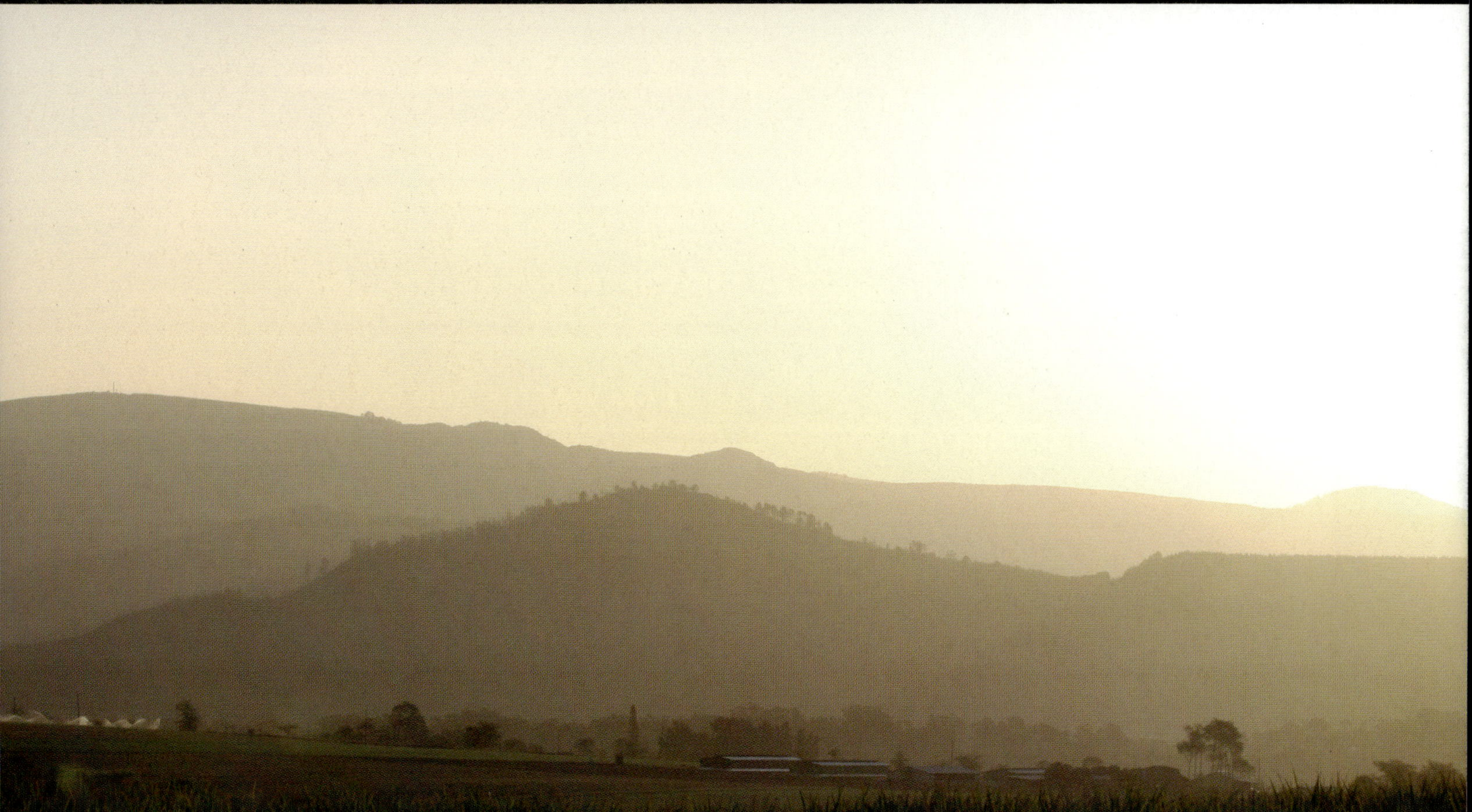

GLOSSARY

#1 "I AM A BOULDER..."

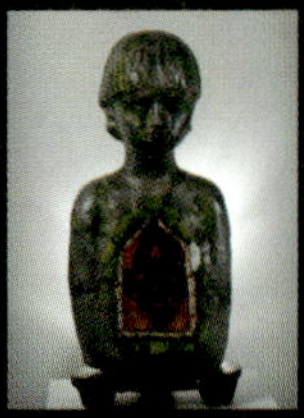

This work reinvents a classic American filmic icon to create an alternate meaning.

Referencing the filmic icon from the Wizard of Oz, "Near the end of the movie, Glenda the good witch appears and instructs Dorothy to tap her ruby heels together three times, while saying the words, 'There's no place like home.' She does this and slowly awakes back in Kansas, still saying the phrase, 'There's no place like home.'"

#2 "I AM SEWN TO THE PAST..."

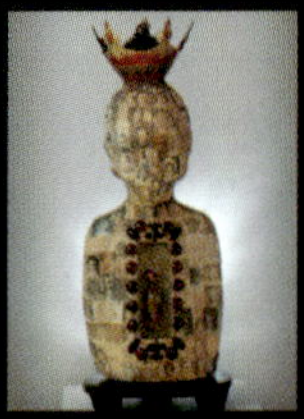

This sculpture references the Medieval Beaver Bestiary as a conjectural illustration of contemporary Post Traumatic Stress Disorder.

"In Christian symbolism the beaver represents chastity, asceticism, and the willingness to sacrifice anything that hinders one's walk with Christ. This is because people once thought that the beaver had a precious medicine bag (castoreum gland) which it would bite off and throw away as excess baggage if pursued. Later it was believed that beavers in flight castrated themselves to avoid capture. Because the beaver gives his position away when he slaps the water with his broad tail, warning his companions of danger, this rodent is a symbol of vigilance, self-sacrifice, and community."[1]

"There is an animal called castor, excessively gentle, whose testes are useful as a remedy in various illnesses. Physiologus explains its [the beaver's] nature by saying that when the hunter shall have found its tracks, he follows in pursuit. The beaver, when he looks back and sees the hunter coming after it, at once tears off its testes with one bite and casts them before the hunter and fleeing thus, escapes. The hunter advancing, however, gathers them up, and pursues no further, but retires."[2]

Posttraumatic Stress Disorder (PTSD): A child or adolescent who experiences a catastrophic event may develop ongoing difficulties known as posttraumatic stress disorder (PTSD). The following are among the symptoms:

- Showing increased alertness to the environment
- Repeating behavior that reminds them of the trauma
- Self-destructive behavior[3]

#3 "I AM WATTLE AND DAUB..."

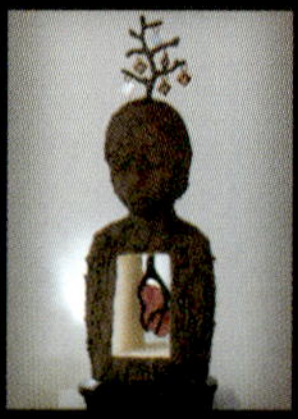

As a standard form of construction in Swaziland, this sculpture relates a physical structure to a universal construct, "the house/people of Swaziland, Africa."

"In building construction, a method of constructing walls in which vertical wooden stakes, or wattles, are woven with horizontal twigs and branches, and then daubed with clay or mud. This method is one of the oldest known for making a weatherproof structure."[4]

#4 "I AM SEALED IN THE WAX OF APATHY..."

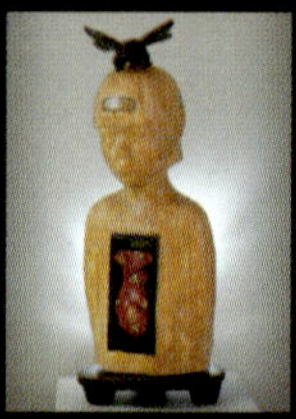

This sculpture employed the use of encaustic during fabrication.

"Encaustic is a painting technique in which pigments are mixed with hot, liquid beeswax. After all of the colors have been applied to the painting surface, a heating element is passed over them until the individual brush or spatula marks fuse into a uniform film. This "burning in" of the colors is an essential element of the true encaustic technique. Encaustic paint-

ing was the commonest technique in the early centuries of the Christian era but fell into disuse in the 8th or 9th century."[5]

Beeswax: The term, commonly used in the phrases mind your own beeswax or none of your beeswax, is an Americanism dating to 1934.[6]

#5 "I AM SCORCHED EARTH AND DRY BONES..."

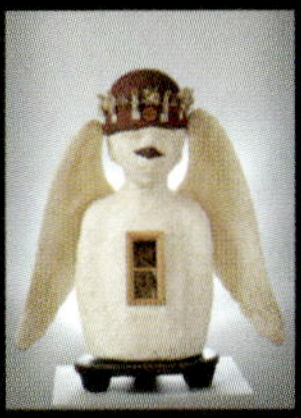

This sculpture uses the concept of the venerated reliquary as homage to the death of the innocent.

Memento Mori: "A Latin phrase meaning 'Remember that you must die.' It is a reminder both of our mortality and of the judgment that will follow our death. Memento mori is also the name given to paintings or sculptures that illustrate the theme of the phrase. Usually featuring a skull, or at least bones, such sculptures were a common feature of tombs in churches in Europe during the late Middle Ages and early modern age. The deceased usually requested that the sculpture be placed on his tomb as a warning to remaining family members (who would frequently visit the tomb) to attend to the good of their souls."[7]

Oracle Bones: Refers to small bones that are used in divination to tell the future. In Swazi society, there remains a strong belief in the ancestors (amadloti), and traditional healers called Sangomas. Generally women, Sangomas are consulted to alleviate physical and mental problems, attend various ceremonies, and act as counselors. When divining, a Sangoma traditionally relies on spirit possession. During the process of divination, a Sangoma will throw (oracle) bones and interpret the patterns in which they fall. The Sangoma or the patient throws the bones, but the ancestors control how they lie. The Sangoma then interprets this metaphor in relation to the patient's life.

Sangomas are steeped in ritual. They work in a sacred healing hut, or Ndumba, where their ancestors reside. They have specific colored cloths to wear to please each ancestor, and often wear the gallbladder of the goat sacrificed at their graduation ceremony in their hair. Wet red clay will often be applied to the head before they perform their rituals.

Traditional healers are routinely consulted by mothers with small children and infants who are suffering from diarrhea. Although not all traditional medicine is harmful, some forms can be deadly. Some healers perform traditional vaccination (kugata) around the baby's naval. A razor blade, usually unsterilized, is used to make shallow cuts and ashes (insiti) of medicines burned over hot coals are rubbed into the resulting cuts. Tragically, this form of medicine has resulted in the spread of HIV/AIDS and other deadly diseases.[8]

Ruarch: Wind, soul, creative breath of God—the mysterious breath of life. Spirit in Hebrew is "ruarch," which means "wind" or "breath." In Ezekiel 37:9 God speaks to Ezekiel in the Valley of the dry bones: "This is what the sovereign Lord says: Come from the four winds, O breath, and breathe on these corpses so that they may live."[9]

#6 "I AM BRICKS AND BLUE..."

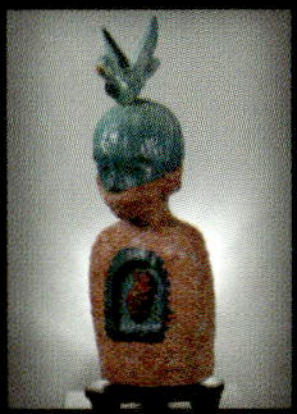

This work functions as visual dichotomy presenting the notion of joy and sorrow cohabitating.

Handwritten around the heart:

"Sympathy" (1899)

I know what the caged bird feels.
Ah me, when the sun is bright on the upland slopes,
when the wind blows soft through the springing grass
and the river floats like a sheet of glass,
when the first bird sings and the first bud ops,
and the faint perfume from its chalice steals.
I know what the caged bird feels.

I know why the caged bird beats his wing
till its blood is red on the cruel bars,
for he must fly back to his perch and cling
when he fain would be on the bow as wing.
And the blood still throbs in the old, old scars
and they pulse again with a keener sting.
I know why he beats his wing.

I know why the caged bird sings.
Ah, me, when its wings are bruised and its bosom sore.
It beats its bars and would be free.
It's not a carol of joy or glee,
but a prayer that it sends from its heart's deep core,
a plea that upward to heaven it flings.
I know why the caged bird sings.

By: Paul Laurence Dunbar[10]

Bluebird: A widely accepted symbol of cheerfulness, happiness, prosperity, hearth and home, good health, new births, the renewal of springtime, etc. Virtually any positive sentiments may be attached to the bluebird.

Jazz Blues: "While blues lyrics often deal with personal adversity, the music itself goes far beyond self-pity. This form of music is visceral, cathartic, and starkly emotional. From unbridled joy to deep sadness, no form of music communicates more genuine emotion.

The blues has deep roots in American history, particularly African-American history. The blues originated on Southern plantations in the 19th Century. Its inventors were slaves, ex-slaves and the descendants of slaves—African-American sharecroppers who sang as they toiled in the cotton and vegetable fields. It's generally accepted that the music evolved from African spirituals, African chants, work songs, field hollers, rural fife and drum music, revivalist hymns, and country dance music.

Most blues music is comprised of 12 bars (or measures). A specific series of notes is also utilized in the blues. The individual parts of this scale are known as the blue notes, also referred to as ('worried notes') blue-like phrasing, or blue riffs."[11]

#7 "I AM COVERED IN THE CEMENT OF BURDEN..."

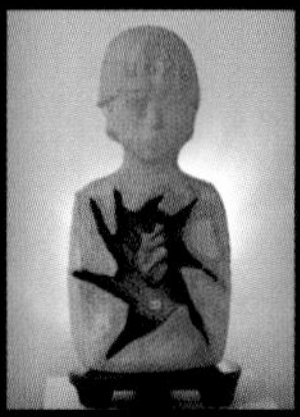

This sculpture is offered as a reminder that there are those who will die unless their burdens are met with fervent intervention.

Cement: "Cement when activated will burn flesh. One problem with cement burns is that, because of the caustic effect, the burn keeps on going even after you no longer have contact with the wet cement."[12]

Goel: In Hebrew, the participle of the verb gaal; "to redeem." It is rendered in the Authorized Version "kinsman," Num. 5:8; Ruth 3:12; 4:1,6,8; "redeemer," Job 19:25; "avenger," Num. 35:12; Deut. 19:6, etc. The Jewish law gave the right of redeeming and repurchasing, as well as of avenging blood, to the next relative, who was accordingly called by this name.[13]

Goel/Kinsman Redeemer: "Provision was made in the Law of Moses for the poor person who was forced to

sell part of his property or himself into slavery. His nearest of kin could step in and "buy back" what his relative was forced to sell (Leviticus 25:48f). The kinsman redeemer was a rich benefactor, or person who freed the debtor by paying the ransom price. "If a fellow countryman of yours becomes so poor he has to sell part of his property, then his nearest kinsman is to come and buy back what his relative has sold" (Leviticus 25:25; cf. Ruth 4:4, 6). The nearest of kin had the responsibility of redeeming his kinsman's lost opportunities. If a person was forced into slavery, his redeemer purchased his freedom."[14]

#8 "I AM A CLOSED DOOR..."

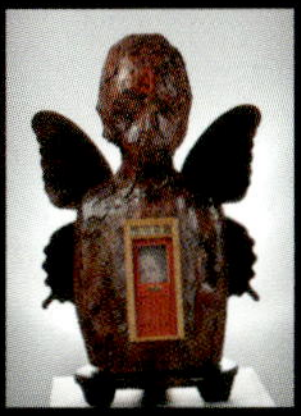

Hiding is a form of self-preservation, but as this sculpture points out, continual defeat will yield to self-incarceration.

"From infancy to until they turned 24, nearly half (48.2 percent) of Swazi women experienced some form of sexual violence, according to the National Survey on Violence Experienced by Female Children and Youths in Swaziland, conducted by the government, UN agencies and non-governmental organizations (NGOs).

Women often submitted to unwanted sex out of fear of physical violence: about 28 percent of girls aged between 13 and 17 experienced physical violence, and the likelihood that they would be assaulted increased as they grew into adulthood, with 33 percent of women aged between 18 and 24 saying they were violence survivors."[15]

Armour: "Armour had to be kept nice, clean and polished. But it also had to be oiled - so that its hinges would let arms and legs to move smoothly and the knight could move swiftly and steadily. Armour rusted from sweat in the fight and in practice. Sweat has acid which makes metal rust even quicker."[16]

#9 "I AM MAMBA AND ORACLE BONES..."

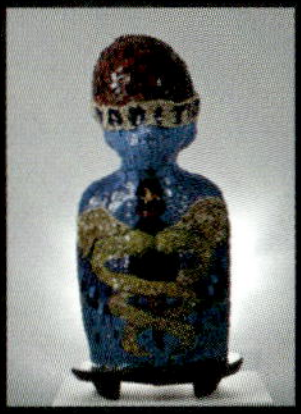

Smalti Tessarae is used on this sculpture which references the coming together of Traditional and Western Medicine in Swaziland.

Smalti Tessarae: "Smalti (the plural of smalto) are specilised mosaic tesserae made from richly coloured glass. Originally developed for Byzantine mosaics, the glass contains metal oxides which produce an almost infinite range of colour possibilities. The molten glass is poured into flat slabs which are then broken into individual smalti with rough, irregular surfaces that may be pitted with air bubbles. A thin layer of gold leaf can be embedded in smalti to produce gold tesserae. Smalti mosaics are normally ungrouted. This allows for the small tiles to capture the light more effectively. Smalti Tessarae was used to depict some of the earliest images of Christ and the Saints."[17]

Artist note: The specific tessarae used on this sculpture are remnants from a centennial medallion created for Bethany First Church of the Nazarene (BFC). The BFC Centennial Medallion symbolically commemorates, among other things, 100 years of mission work.

Black Mamba: "They get their name not from their skin color, which tends to be olive to gray, but rather from the blue-black color of the inside of their mouth, which they display when threatened."[18]

"The black mamba is Africa's deadliest snake. Untreated, its bite has a fatality rate of 100 percent, making it a killer among killers on a continent where it

each year, and the residents of Swaziland in southern Africa have suffered losses for generations. With essentially no access to anti-venom, many people turn to traditional healers for help, but their herbal remedies always fail, leaving Swazis feeling fearful and defenseless against one of their nation's most infamous killers."[19]

Oracle Bones: See #5 Glossary

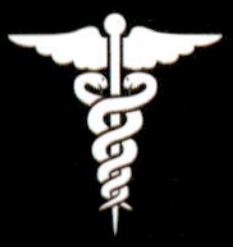

Caduceus: "Many 'medical' organizations use a symbol of a short rod entwined by two snakes and topped by a pair of wings, which is actually the caduceus, or magic wand, of the Greek god Hermes (Roman Mercury), messenger of the gods." The words caduity & caducous imply temporal, perishable, and senile, while the medical profession espouses renewal, vitality, and health. The link between the caduceus carried by Hermes (Mercury) and medicine seems to have arisen by the seventh century A.D., when Hermes was linked with alchemy.[20]

#10 "I AM SHATTERED GLASS AND TRANSPARENT HEART..."

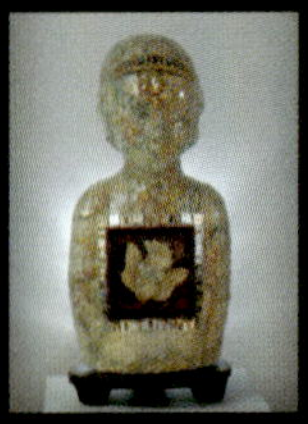

With brokenness covering a torn and confused world, the piece is a reminder that the notion of "over there" is a dangerous fallacy.

Aurora: The Roman goddess of the morning red, or dawn, who brings up the light of day from the east. When her son Memnon was going to fight against Achilles, she asked Hephaestus to give her arms for him. When Memnon was killed, legend has it that her tears fell down in the form of morning dew. She is often depicted with wings and a full flowing gown.[21]

#11 "I AM A JUTE COCOON AND A NEW WING..."

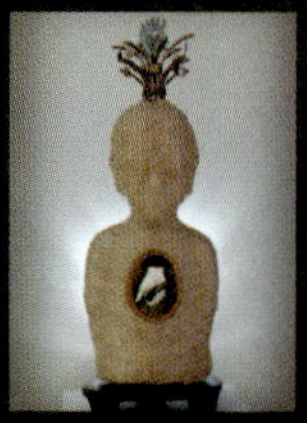

This cocoon sculpture serves as a signifier of our earthly cast—a temporary shelter for the labor of the soul.

Jute: Jute is an extremely versatile vegetable fiber known for its strength and durability. It is derived from a relative of the hemp plant. Jute fibers are long, varying from 1.5 to 3.5 meters, and good quality Jute has a golden sheen to it, earning it the nickname "the golden fiber". The fibers are spun into yarn, and then woven into a fabric, which is known in the US as burlap. Jute is a totally biodegradable, extremely strong, durable, and inexpensive fiber.

Artist note: While in the market in Manzini, I was fascinated to watch as the women would carefully pull jute fibers out of old burlap bags and recycle them for their crafts.

Cocoon: The purpose of a cocoon is to envelop for protection from a harsh or unfriendly environment; to retreat as if into a cocoon, as for security from a harsh or unfriendly environment.[22]

Metamorphoun: Greek: metamorphosis meaning a profound change in form from one stage to the next in the life history of an organism, as from the caterpillar to the pupa and from the pupa to the adult butterfly.[23]

#12 "I AM THE GOLDEN ORATOR..."

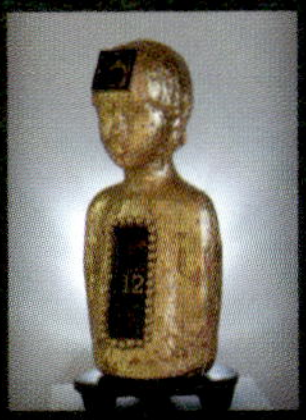

This work is a symbol of us all—storytellers—marked with evidence of the lives we've lived and the paths we've traveled

Vestige: A mark, trace, or visible evidence of something that is no longer present or in existence.[24]

Mgaba: A form of traditional healing originating from the Zulu and used in Swaziland, in which cutaneous implantation—small incisions made with a sharpened knife or razor blade—is used. Once the incisions have been made the muti (traditional medicine) is then brushed over the cuts to introduce it rapidly into the blood.[25]

Sojourner: Noun: a temporary stay. Verb: to stay for a time in a place; live temporarily.[26]

Sojourner Truth: Born Isabella Baumfree, in 1843, she took the name Sojourner Truth, believing this to be on the instructions of the Holy Spirit and became a traveling preacher (the meaning of her new name). In the late 1840s she connected with the abolitionist movement, becoming a popular speaker. In 1850, she also began speaking on woman suffrage. She is remembered as a United States abolitionist and feminist who was freed from slavery and became a leading advocate of the abolition of slavery and for the rights of women.

"I am not going to die, I am going
home like a shooting star."
— Sojourner Truth.

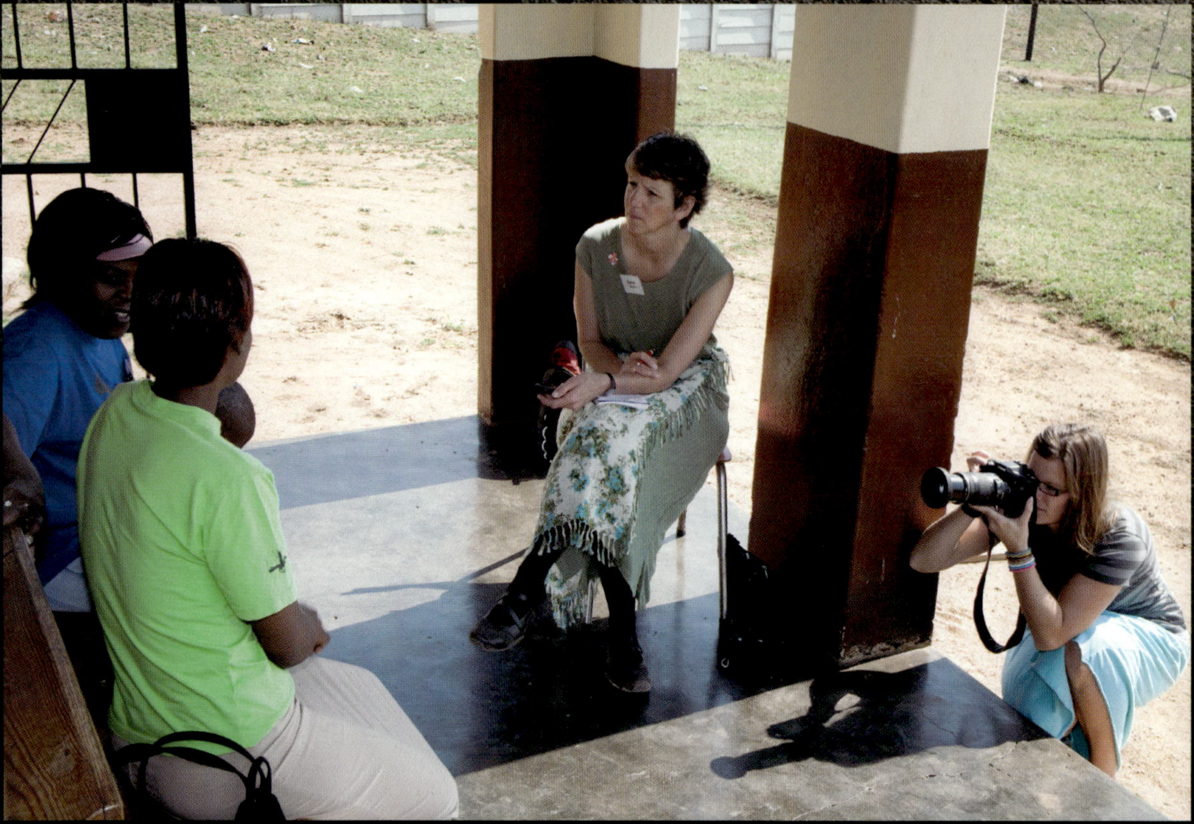

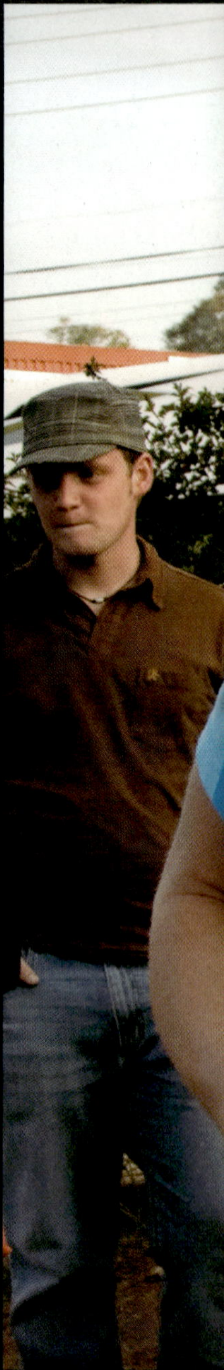

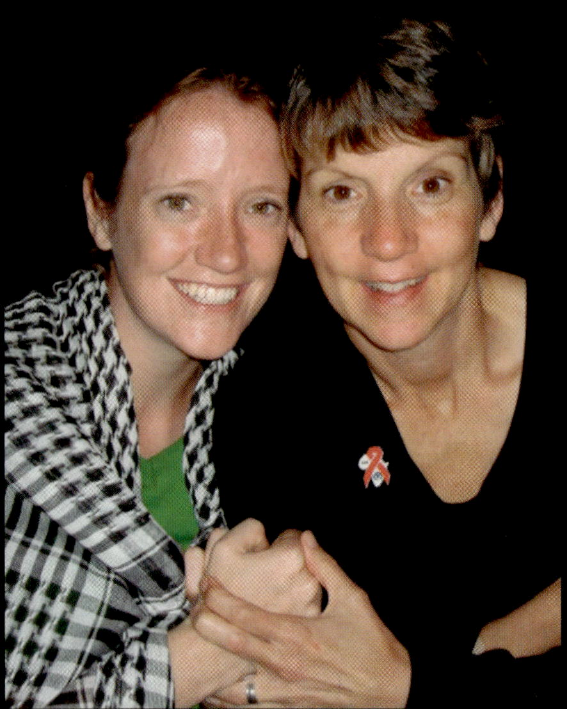

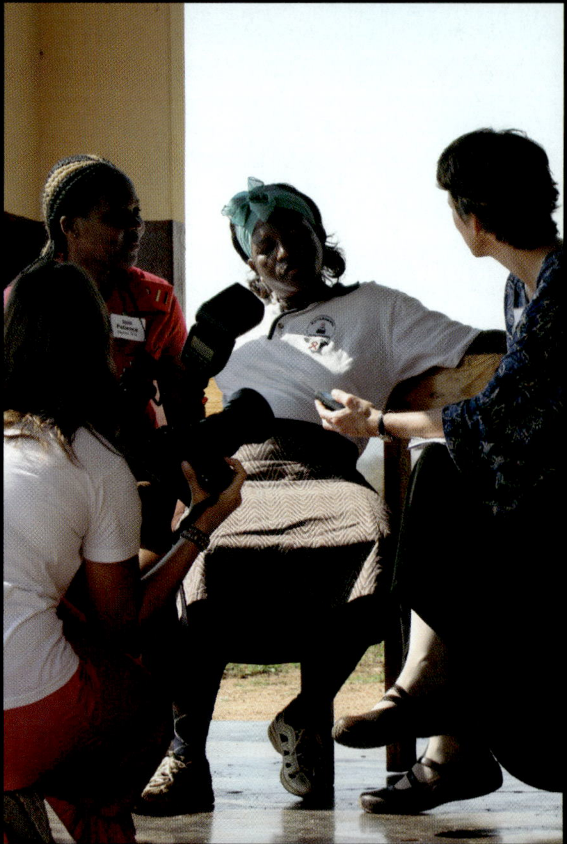

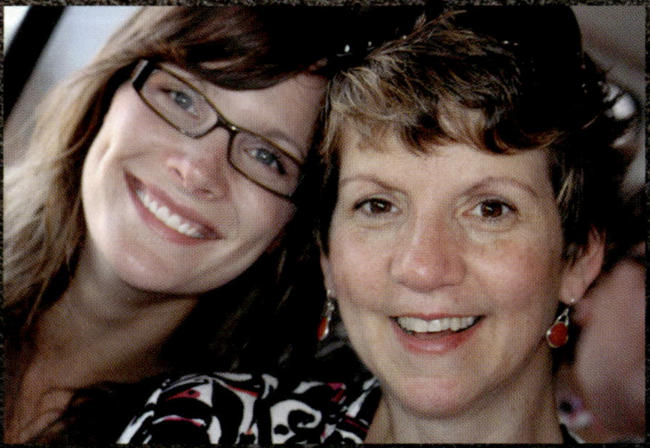

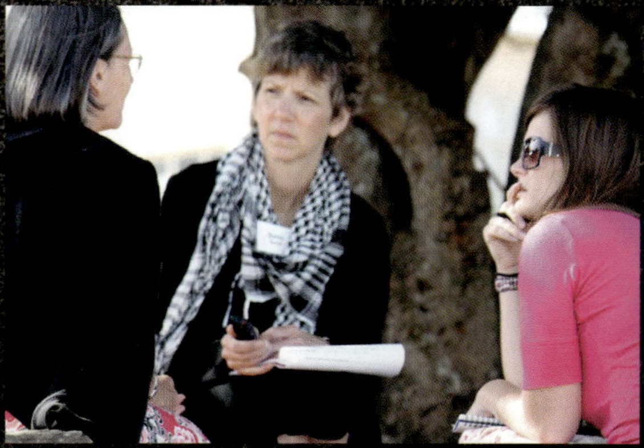

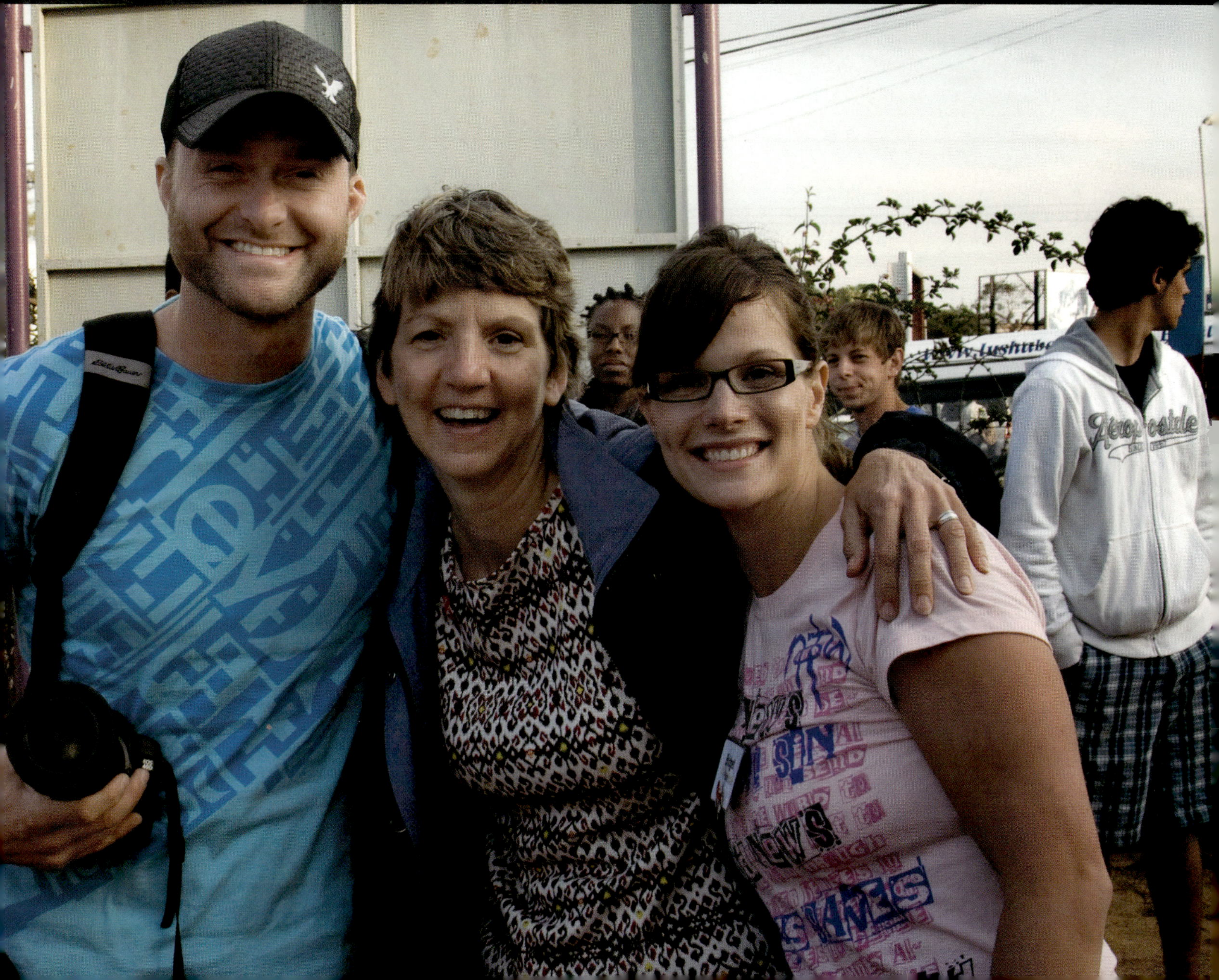
Aeropostale

SOURCES

Information on Swaziland

1. http://www.unep.org/ik/Pages.asp?id=About%20IK
2. http://pubs.acs.org/doi/pdfplus/10.1021/bk-2009-1021.ch003
3. http://www.everyculture.com/Africa-Middle-East/Swazi-Religion-and-Expressive-Culture.html

Glossary

1. Tucker, Suzetta. "Christ Story Beaver Page." Christ Story Christian Bestiary. 1997. http://ww2.netnitco.net/users/legend01/beaver.htm.
2. CAHR, CHARLS, 'Le Physiologus ou bestiaire', in: CAHIER, CHAR S, and MARTN, ARTHR, Melanges d'Arch6ologie, Pars, Poussielgue-Rusand, 1851-56; 2, 85-100, 106-232; 3, 203-88; 4, 55-87.
3. Copyright ©2009 - American Academy of Child Adolescent Psychiatry. All Rights Reserved.
4. "wattle and daub." Encyclopedia Britannica. 2010. Encyclopedia Britannica Online. 14 Jul. 2010 <http://www.britannica.com/EBchecked/topic/637711/wattle-and-daub>.
5. "encaustic painting." Encyclopedia Britannica. 2010. Encyclopedia Britannica Online. 14 Jul. 2010 <http://www.britannica.com/EBchecked/topic/186438/encaustic-painting>.
6. Wordorigins.com: Copyright 1997-2010, by David Wilton
7. http://catholicism.about.com/od/history/g/Memento_Mori.htm,
8. http://www.stwr.org/health-education-shelter/traditional-healers-mothers-and-childhood-diarrheal-disease-in-swaziland.html
9. Encyclopedia Britannica. 2010. Encyclopedia Britannica Online. 14 Jul. 2010 <http://www.britannica.com/EBchecked/topic/407972/nefesh>.
10. This poem was published in Lyrics of the Hearthside by Dodd, Mead and Company in 1899. It was this poem that inspired the title to Maya Angelou's autobiography I Know Why The Caged Bird Sings. Another poem entitled "Sympathy" appeared in his first book, Oak and Ivy, that he distributed at the 1893 World's Columbian Exposition in Chicago.
11. http://www.allaboutjazz.com/php/article.php?id=18724
12. http://www.associatedcontent.com/article/2123935/cement_burns_can_hurt.html?cat=6
13. http://onlinedictionary.datasegment.com/word/goel
14. Quotations designated (NET) are from the NET Bible® copyright ©1996-2006 by Biblical Studies Press, L.L.C. http://www.bible.org/. All rights reserved.
15. SWAZILAND: Two-thirds of women beaten and abused, Humanitarian news and analysis a project of the UN Office for the Coordination of Humanitarian Affairs Copyright © IRIN 2010. All rights reserved.
16. http://www.fencingforkids.com/index.php?option=com_content&view=article&id=77:article-history-rust&catid=37:news-qna&Itemid=37
17. http://www.thejoyofshards.co.uk/glossary/smalti.shtml

19. http://www.pbs.org/wnet/nature/episodes/black-mamba/introduction/5260/
20. uchomp.bsd.uchicago.edu/documents/Asclapia.doc
21. http://www.theoi.com/Titan/Eos.html
22. http://www.thefreedictionary.com/cocoon
23. http://dictionary.reference.com/browse/metamorphosis
24. http://dictionary.reference.com/
25. http://library.thinkquest.org/27209/Healing.htm
26. http://dictionary.reference.com/browse/sojourn

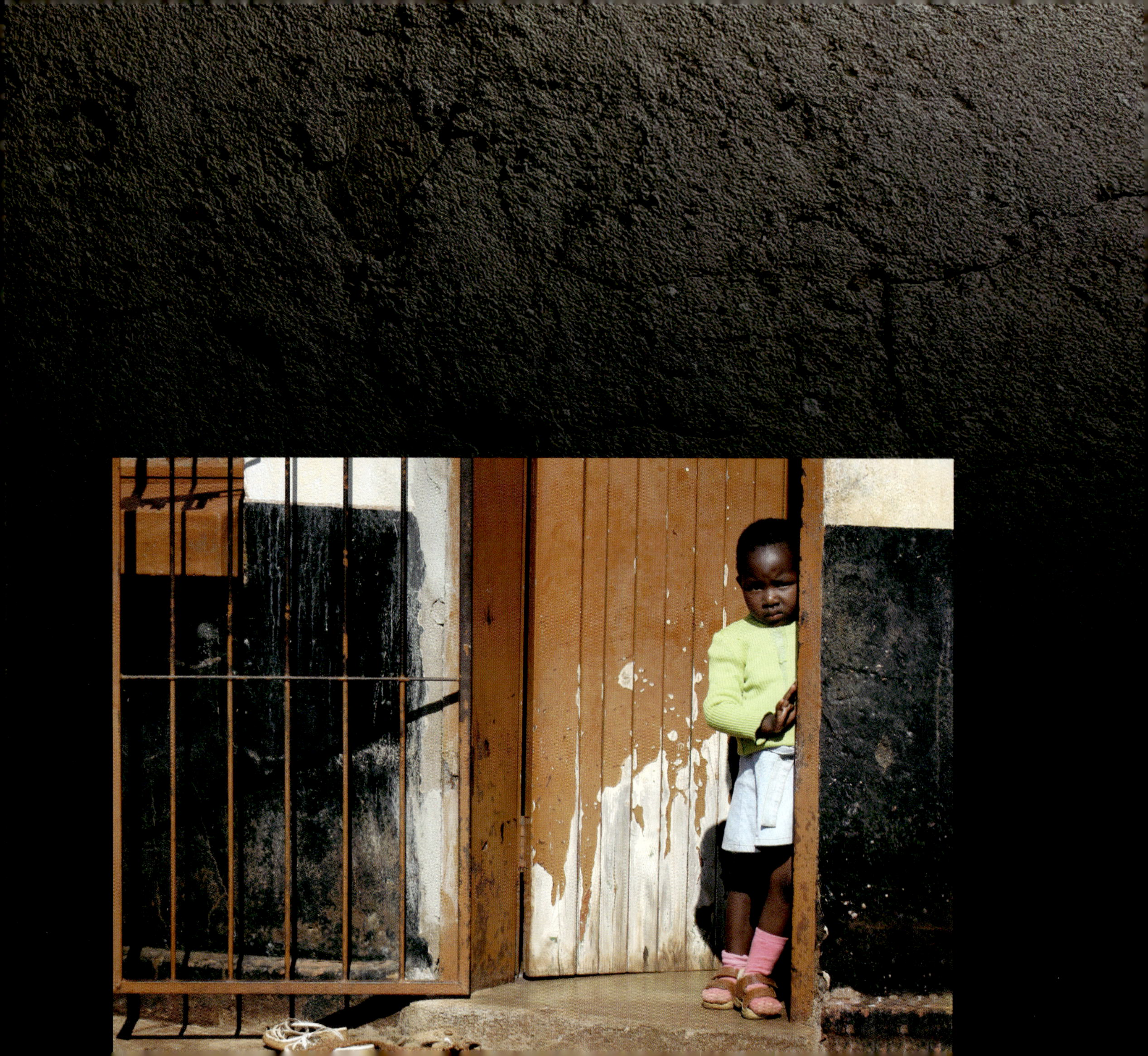